WORDS

SOME WISE ...
SOME OTHERWISE

by John Leslie

Illustrations by Rafi

ISBN: 978-0-578-09791-6

Printed in the United
States of America
Little Red Hen Book. First
printing December, 2011.

The little
RedHen
BOOK GROUP

Little Red Hen
Book Group
Spring, Texas

WORDS

Dedication

To my *Mexican and Margarita* friends.
You continue to inspire me!

About the Author

John Leslie, the retired President of The Leslie Corporation. started a second career of service to others. He now is a volunteer chaplain, and recently completed a term on the churches-sponsored Northwest Assistance Ministries Board of Directors, and still serves that organization as a counselor. He is a cancer survivor and a CanCare volunteer, working with others who are undergoing Prostate Cancer treatment. He has been a long-time member of the CanCare Board of Representatives.

He is an Elder in the Presbyterian Church. As a Presbyterian lay pastor, he served as Chairman of the Board of the Presbyterian Outreach to Patients, a group ministering to hospital patients throughout the Houston area. He recently served seniors of Texas as a member of "The Silver-Haired Legislature," a group which mirrors the regular legislature but works exclusively for seniors. He has been an active member of the Harris County Area Agency on Aging.

He lectures on the topic, " Preparing for the End of Life," which is based on his book, *I'm Getting Older, But I'm Not Dead Yet,* teaches adult learning classes on contemporary morality and ethical issues. He is a motivational speaker on mentoring and modern morality themes.

This book, *Words, Some Wise, Some Otherwise,* is the third book in a series of four.

His fourth book, *"We Were the Perfect Pair, But You Died. What Do I Do Now?"* is scheduled for publication in late 2012.

He is a 1953 graduate of the University of Arkansas. He and his wife, Janice reside in Houston, Texas.

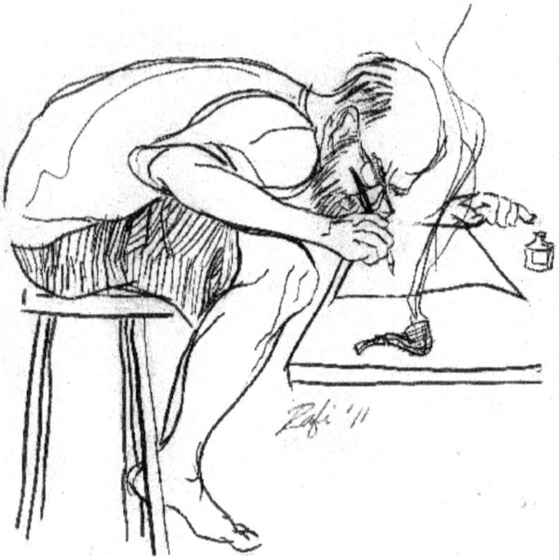
Rafi '11

About the Artist and Illustrations

Ron Folsom says he has always enjoyed all the arts. However, following his retirement from a career within the Graphics Design industry, both as a business owner and corporate employee, he became a full-time artist, concentrating on pen and pencil drawing, painting with acrylics and computer graphics design. His paintings have been featured in several showings in the Houston area.

Ron uses the pseudonym, "Rafi," to sign his work. He says he does so because he has a hard time talking about himself. "Using the name, 'Rafi' is like there's a third party out there I can talk about. Also, it's my initials with an 'i' added."

This is the second book he has illustrated for John Leslie. The first, *"Book of Toasts,"* received critical acclaim for his artistic renderings.

Illustrations Plates (with explanations by Rafi)

Page 2.   **Watch your Thoughts.** This one indicates that what you think you see may not be correct. Is she at a bar or home? Is someone else there? You can look at it anyway you want and be right.

Page 4.   **Need Regular Weeding.** Believing there are Angels standing by and removing the weeds in our lives helps us all get by.

Page 6.   **Style.** What envisages style more than a black-tie event?

Page 8.   **Strive for Balance.** I like to think Angels can have fun too. Using us humans as part of a see-saw might help get our lives balanced again.

Page 10.   **Life Is Not Fair.** You can look at this as the departing couple leaving the oarsman a bad tip or, perhaps, the old man walked off with his girlfriend? Who can say what's fair or not?

Page 14.   **Season with Tranquility.** It takes time for things to become comfortable. This drawing is based on a painting by Paul Jacobsen. When I first saw the original painting, I was reminded of my Dad in his favorite chair, listening to a Cardinals baseball game. He left me too soon.

Page 20.   **Internal Monologue or Talking to Yourself.** My wife talks to herself. She wins every argument. Of course I don't...do I Rafi?

Page 24.   **A Snail's Pace.** This was fun to do. I'm really out of the box on this one. Two snails racing? What better way to show us to "Take Time."

Page 30.   **A Spouse in Trouble.** This is such a funny story. I do not think the art can do it justice. It would be fun to try some of these at our local discount store!

Page 34.   **Anybody Can Be a Golfer.** To me, Golf is the greatest game that has ever been played. And anybody can try to play it . . . even a geek.

W O R D S

Preface

This book is one of a series of four that relate to living and dying. Judged by the book titles, it may be difficult to imagine them fitting into a "living and dying" category. In the outline, this book about the words we use to make life meaningful, is the second of the four.

Our lives are pretty much divided into thirds: the first third was your childhood, early youth and education.

The second period represents the time you graduated from school, got a job, married, had children, and educated them.

The third period was your retirement. You may have skidded into retirement, getting ready for it a little at a time. Or you may have been forced into retirement by an unforgiving company. Or you have been without work for a long, long time, and finally, took the additional income from Social Security and called yourself "retired."

It's this last third of life that is of interest to me and my aging friends. And that's the period I've chosen to write about. For lots of reasons, this last third seems to be lasting longer and longer, so there are a lot of things to do and think about.

Living is, for most of us, just putting one foot ahead of the other. We try to plan, and sometimes we succeed. We strive for excellence; sometimes we don't quite make it. We do the best we can. Luckily, there are times when we lay back and just enjoy what we have. "Words" is that kind of a book. Almost all the stuff in it is intended for fun reading. Some famous people's words are in it, some famous writers' words are included, and lots of authors you've never heard of made contributions. Like life, things happen.

Several of my friends have said this is an easy-reading book, the kind best read in spurts! Each article is, on purpose, relatively short. Only a few of the pieces are intended to seriously jiggle your thought processes. I hope the ones on Creation do.

My fourth book is about overcoming the trauma following the death of a life partner. It's now a series of lectures—trying out the ideas on real people, persons who are the living half of a pair. Look for it next year (it's due to be published in 2012), after it has been thoroughly tested in reality.

Here's the cycle of life outline and the book that seemed to fit:

Celebration of Life:
"John Leslie's Book of Toasts"

Life's Journey:
"Words...Some Wise, Some Otherwise"

Preparing for the End of Life:
"I'm Getting Older, but I'm Not Dead Yet!"

Life As A Survivor:
"We Were the Perfect Pair, but You Died. Now What Do I Do?"

Each of these books was developed in response to a need. It could have been a friend going through a personal crisis, experiencing a relationship issue, or trying to make a connection with another...something was the tipping point that caused me to want to get my brain around a topic.

I hope your Life's Journey is a pleasant one and that I've contributed in a small measure to your joy

John Leslie

WORDS

Contents

WORDS

𝕎🄾🆁🄳🆂

PERSONAL, VERY PERSONAL

Watch your Thoughts
Pencil drawing on 8x10 drawing paper
© 2011 Rafi

Hesychios the Priest wrote in the 8th or 9th century, "Guard your mind and you will not be harassed by temptations. But if you fail to guard it, accept patiently whatever trial comes."

Your Legacy

Watch your thoughts, for they become words.

Watch your words, for they become actions.

Watch your actions, for they become habits.

Watch your habits, for they become character.

Watch your character, for it becomes your legacy.

These instructions are attributed to both Frank Outlaw and Charles Reade.

Need Regular Weeding

Graphite Stick on 8x 10 drawing paper

© 2011 Rafi

❧ Growing Up ☙

Be gentle with yourself.

Growing up is a process that may take some time and effort. Core beliefs are often deeply rooted and need regular weeding. They do not need to be obsessed about, or even given much attention to, but they do need to be weeded.

Pull the weeds. Then focus on the roses.

Attributed to Victoria Loveland Coen, RScP

Style — computer generated © 2011 Rafi

WORDS

Being the best person you can be is determined by lots of things, one of which is how you treat others. People are like snowflakes; every one of us is different. "Best person" means something to each of us, but not the same to all of us. Call whatever you are day in, day out, "your style." If you haven't yet made up your mind what your style is, here are some guidelines.

Your "STYLE"

The rules you live by define your "style." Your style defines your character, how you think about yourself and how you treat others.

Carl Sagan, the late science populist and author of the book, *Billions and Billions*, identified 6 styles (he called them "Rules that people live by"). He wrote about the rules in the November 1993 edition of Parade Magazine.

You may see your friends in these descriptions...and yourself.

The Iron Rule—Do unto others as you like, before they do it unto you.

The Silver Rule—Do not do unto others what you would not have them do unto you.

The Golden Rule—Do unto others as you would have them do unto you.

The Tin Rule—Suck up to those above you, and intimidate those below (it's the Golden Rule for superiors and the Iron Rule for inferiors).

The Nepotism Rule—Give precedence in all things to close relatives, and do as you like with others.

The Bronze Rule—Repay kindness with kindness, but evil with justice. Tit for Tat.

Here's how The Bronze Rule, the best of them all, works:
- Be friendly at first meetings.
- Do not envy.
- Be generous; forgive your enemy if he forgives you. Be neither a tyrant nor a patsy.
- Retaliate proportionally to an intentional injury (within the constraints of the rule of law, of course).
- Make your behavior fairly clear and consistent (although not perfectly clear).

*This choice of behavior is also discussed in Robert Axelrod's book, **The Evolution of Cooperation.** He describes the choices in the section he calls, "The Prisoner's Dilemma."*

Strive for Balance

Pen & ink with wash on 8x10 drawing paper

© 2011 Rafi

WORDS

Everyone has an idea or two about the way you should live. They mean well and we should listen to what they say...they may be right.

Some Rules to Govern How We Live

These are rules from church friends

Strive for balance in your life.

Don't work too much...or too little.

Spend time with your family and loved ones.

Exercise, sleep, and eat...properly.

Participate in a Faith Group at church.

Really listen to people when you talk with them.

Hug someone every day.

Always work hard and find pleasure in what you do.

Smile, be yourself.

Have goals.

Consider the consequences of your dreams and actions.

Be responsible, especially to yourself.

Understand and manage your personal finances.

Life is Not fair
Pen & ink on 8x10 drawing paper
© 2011 Rafi

WORDS

As we live life, we learn a lesson or two. Here's what Regina Bret has learned so far.

Lessons Life Taught Me
(According to Regina Brett)

Life isn't fair, but it's still good.

When in doubt, just take the next small step.

Life is too short to waste time hating anyone.

Don't take yourself so seriously. No one else does.

Pay off your credit cards every month.

You don't have to win every argument. Agree to disagree.

Cry with someone. It's more healing than crying alone.

It's OK to get angry with God. He can take it.

Save for retirement, starting with your first paycheck.

When it comes to chocolate, resistance is futile.

Make peace with your past so it won't screw up the present.

It's OK to let your children see you cry

Don't compare your life to others. You have no idea what their journey is all about.

If a relationship has to be a secret, you shouldn't be in it.

Everything can change in the blink of an eye. But don't worry; God never blinks.

Take a deep breath. It calms the mind.

Get rid of anything that isn't useful, beautiful or joyful.

Whatever doesn't kill you really does make you stronger.

When it comes to going after what you love in life, don't take "no" for an answer.

Burn the candles, use the nice sheets, and wear the fancy lingerie. Don't save them for a special occasion.

Today is special. Over prepare, and then go with the flow.

Be eccentric now. Don't wait for old age to wear purple.

The most important sex organ is the brain.

No one is in charge of your happiness, except you.

Frame every so-called disaster with these words: "In five years, will this matter?"

Always choose life.

Forgive everyone everything.

What other people think of you is none of your business.

Time heals almost everything. Give time, time.

However good or bad a situation is, it will change.

Your job won't take care of you when you are sick. Your friends will. Stay in touch.

Believe in miracles.

God loves you because of whom God is, not because of anything you did or didn't do.

Don't audit life. Show up and make the most of it now.

Growing old beats the alternative: dying young.

Your children get only one childhood. Make it memorable. All that truly matters in the end is that you loved.

Get outside every day. Miracles are waiting everywhere.

WORDS

If we all threw our problems in a pile and saw everyone else's, we'd grab ours back.

Envy is a waste of time. You already have all you need.

The best is yet to come.

No matter how you feel, get up, dress up and show up.

Yield.

Life is not the way it's supposed to be. It's the way it is. The way you cope with it is what makes the difference

Ms. Brett worked for The Plain Dealer Newspaper in Cleveland, Ohio at the time she wrote this.

Season with Tranquility
Graphite Stick on 8x10 drawing paper
© 2011 Rafi

Things It Took Me 30 Years To Learn

By Dave Barry
Actually, it took Dave more than 30 years…and he says there are
some things he's still working on.

Never under any circumstances take a sleeping pill and a laxative on the same night.

If you had to identify, in one word, the reason why the human race has not achieved and never will achieve its full potential, that word would be "meetings."

There is a very fine line between "hobby" and "mental illness."

People who want to share their religious views with you almost never want you to share yours.

And when God, who created the entire universe with all of its glories, decides to deliver a message to humanity, he will not use as his messenger a person on cable TV with a bad hairstyle.

You should not confuse your career with your life.

No matter what happens, somebody will find a way to take it too seriously.

Take out the fortune before you eat the cookie.

The most powerful force in the universe is gossip.

You will never find anybody who can give you a clear and compelling reason why we observe daylight savings time.

The one thing that unites all human beings, regardless of age, gender, religion, economic status or ethnic background, is that deep down inside we all believe that we are above average drivers.

A person who is nice to you, but rude to the waiter, is not a nice person.

Your friends love you anyway.

ADVICE I WISH I'D BEEN GIVEN...AND TAKEN

THE QUICKEST WAY TO DOUBLE YOUR MONEY IS TO FOLD IT IN HALF AND PUT IT BACK IN YOUR POCKET.

IF AT FIRST YOU DON'T SUCCEED, SKY DIVING IS NOT FOR YOU

If you tell the truth, you don't have to remember anything

Don't be irreplaceable.
If you can't be replaced,
YOU CAN'T BE
PROMOTED.

NEVER MISS
A GOOD
CHANCE TO
SHUT UP

WORDS

Experience is something you don't get until just after you need it.

GIVE A MAN A FISH AND HE WILL EAT FOR A DAY. TEACH HIM HOW TO FISH, AND HE WILL SIT IN A BOAT AND DRINK BEER ALL DAY.

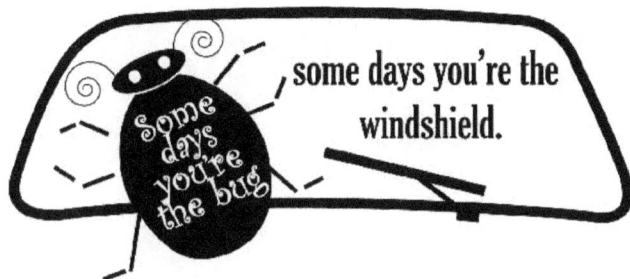

some days you're the bug

some days you're the windshield.

Everybody seems normal . . . UNTIL YOU GET TO KNOW THEM

**Do not walk behind me,
for I may not lead.**

**Do not walk ahead of me,
for I may not follow.**

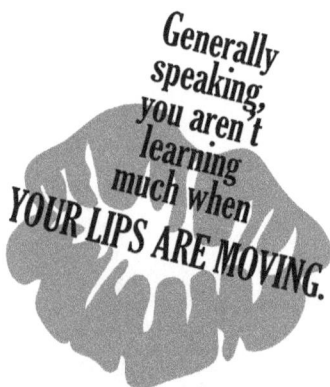

Duct tape is like The Force. It has a light side and a dark side, and it holds the universe together

Generally speaking, you aren't learning much when YOUR LIPS ARE MOVING.

Always remember
that y●u're unique.
Just like
every●ne
else.

WORDS

Do not walk beside me either.

Just pretty much leave me the hell alone.

If you lend someone $20 and never see that person again, it was probably worth it.

If you think nobody cares if you are alive, . . .

TRY MISSING A COUPLE CAR PAYMENTS

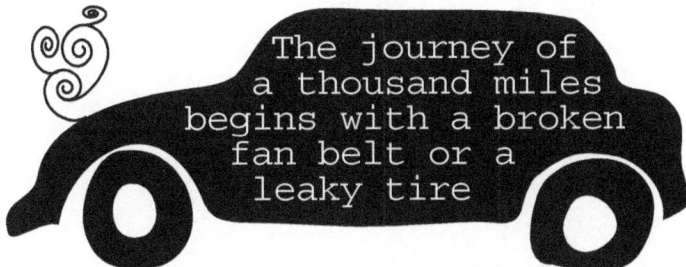

The journey of a thousand miles begins with a broken fan belt or a leaky tire

Internal Monoloque: Talking to Yourself
Pen & ink with wash on 8x10 drawing paper
© 2011 Rafi

WORDS

Talking To Yourself

Wisdom is the reward you get for a lifetime of listening when you'd have preferred to talk.

People of lesser ability sometimes achieve outstanding success because they don't know when to quit.

Keep skunks, bankers and lawyers at a distance.

Life is simpler when you plow around the stump.

A bumble bee is considerably faster than a John Deere tractor.

Words that soak into your ears are whispered...not yelled.

Meanness just doesn't happen overnight.

Forgive your enemies. It messes up their heads.

Do not corner something that you know is meaner than you.

It doesn't take a very big person to carry a grudge.

You cannot unsay a cruel word.

Every path has a few puddles.

When you wallow with pigs, expect to get dirty.

The best sermons are lived, not preached.

Most of the stuff people worry about ain't ever gonna happen anyway.

Don't judge folks by their relatives.

Remember that silence is sometimes the best answer.

Live a good, honorable life. Then when you get older and think back, you'll enjoy it a second time.

Don't interfere with something that's not bothering you.

Timing has a lot to do with the outcome of a rain dance.

If you find yourself in a hole, the first thing to do is stop digging.

Sometimes you get, and sometimes you get got.

The biggest troublemaker you'll probably ever have to deal with watches you from the mirror every morning.

Letting the cat out of the bag is a whole lot easier than putting it back in.

If you get to thinking you're a person of some influence, try ordering somebody else's dog around.

Live simply. Love generously. Care deeply. Speak kindly. Leave the rest to God.

A sharp tongue can cut my own throat.

If I want my dreams to come true, I mustn't oversleep.

Of all the things I wear, my expression is the most important.

The best vitamin for making friends. . . B1.

The happiness of my life depends on the quality of my thoughts.

The heaviest thing I can carry is a grudge.

One thing I can give and still keep...is my word.

If I lack the courage to start, I have already finished.

One thing I can't recycle is wasted time.

Ideas won't work unless I do.

Good judgment comes from experience, and a lot of that comes from bad judgment.

The pursuit of happiness is the chase of a lifetime!

W O R D S

It is never too late to become what I might have been.

Sometimes we are so caught up in who's right and who's wrong that we forget what's right and wrong.

Sometimes we just don't realize what real friendship means until it is too late.

Surely it is no coincidence that the word "listen" is an anagram of the word "silent."

There is so much pollution in the air now that if it weren't for our lungs there'd be no place to put it all.

Some people pay a compliment as if they expect a receipt.

Doug Larson is the author of some of these wise words; the other authors are named "Unknown."

A Snail's Pace

Pen & ink on 8x10 drawing paper

© 2011 Rafi

Take Time

Take time to think; it is the source of power.

Take time to play; it is the secret of perpetual youth.

Take time to read; it is the fountain of wisdom.

Take time to pray; it is the greatest power on earth.

Take time to love and be loved; it is a God-given privilege.

Take time to be friendly; it is the road to happiness.

Take time to laugh; it is the music of the soul.

Take time to give; it is too short a day to be selfish.

Take time to work; it is the price of success.

Take time to save; it is the foundation of your future.

Take time to be quiet; it is the opportunity to seek God.

Take time to be aware; it is the opportunity to help others.

Take time to dream; it is what the future is made of.

The author of this good advice is unknown.

So You Thought You Knew Everything?

The liquid inside young coconuts can be used as **a substitute for blood plasma.**

No piece of paper can be folded in half **more than seven times.**

Donkeys kill more people annually **than plane crashes or shark attacks.** (So, watch your Ass!).

You burn more calories sleeping **than watching television.**

Oak trees do not produce acorns **until they are 50 years of age or older.**

The first product to have a bar code **was Wrigley's gum.**

The King of Hearts is the only king **without a moustache.**

American Airlines saved $40,000 in 1987 by eliminating one olive **from each salad served in first-class.**

Venus is the only planet that rotates clockwise. **(Since Venus is normally associated with women, does this tell you that women are going in the 'right' direction?)**

Apples, not caffeine, **are more efficient at waking you up in the morning.**

Most dust particles in your house are made from **dead skin!**

The first owner of the Marlboro Company died **of lung cancer. So did the first 'Marlboro Man.'**

A duck's quack doesn't echo, **and no one knows why.**

Pearls melt **in vinegar!**

WORDS

It is possible to lead a cow upstairs...**but not downstairs**

Dentists have recommended that a **toothbrush be kept at least six feet away from a toilet** to avoid airborne particles resulting from the flush.

And the best for last: **turtles can breathe through their butts!**

So...now you know everything!   You'll be the delight of every party!

Analyze This,
Or At Least Make A Rough Guess

When they say, "Analyze this," or "Analyze that," it's supposed to indicate that the result of your analysis will tell you the correct thing to do next.

Most of us probably think analysis is a methodology used only by engineers and scientists. But everyone can use the technique.

And what is analysis? Eugene M. Schwartz, the author of the seminal book, "Breakthrough Advertising," has described the concept in a way that is useful to all of us. He says **"analysis is a series of measuring rods, checkpoints, and signpost questions that show you where a particular force is going, and either enable you to get there first or avoid going at all."**

Not bad.

He goes on to say that analysis is **"a series of rough guesses, based on past successes, which enable you to cut through the surface of a problem to see what makes it tick. Analysis is the art of asking the right questions and letting the problem dictate the right answers. It is the technique of the break through.**

"And analysis can be learned just as surely as grammar, mathematics or spelling."

Now, analyze your life!

HUSBANDS, Wives & CHILDREN

A Spouse Problem

Pen and ink on 8x10 drawing paper

© 2011 Rafi

If you're still working, this little article will give you some great ideas on ways to fill up your time after you leave the workaday world!

You Won't Believe What Happens In Retirement

After I retired, my wife insisted that I accompany her on her trips to Super Discount Store. Unfortunately, like most men, I found shopping boring and preferred to get in and get out quickly. Equally unfortunate, my wife is like most women: she loves to browse.

Yesterday my dear wife received the following letter from the local Super Discount Store:

Dear Mrs. Harris,

Over the past six months, your husband has caused quite a commotion in our store. We cannot tolerate this behavior and have been forced to ban both of you from the store. Our complaints against your husband, Mr. Harris, are listed below and are documented by our video surveillance cameras.

June 15: He took 24 boxes of condoms and randomly put them in other people's carts when they weren't looking.

July 2: Set all the alarm clocks in Housewares to go off at 5 minute intervals.

July 7: He made a trail of tomato juice on the floor leading to the women's rest room.

July 19: Walked up to an employee and told her in an official voice, 'Code 3 in Housewares. Get on it right away.' This caused the employee to leave her assigned station and receive a reprimand from her Supervisor that in turn resulted with a union grievance, causing management to lose time and costing the company money.

August 4: Went to the Service Desk and tried to put a bag of M&M's on layaway.

August 14: Moved a 'CAUTION WET FLOOR' sign to a carpeted area.

August 15: Set up a tent in the camping department and told the children shoppers he'd invite them in if they would bring pillows and blankets from the bedding department to which twenty children obliged.

August 23: When a clerk asked if they could help him he began crying and screamed, 'Why can't you people just leave me alone?' EMTs were called.

September 4: Looked right into the security camera and used it as a mirror while he picked his nose.

September 10: While handling guns in the hunting department, he asked the clerk where the antidepressants were.

October 3: Darted around the store suspiciously while loudly humming the 'Mission Impossible' theme.

October 6: In the auto department, he practiced his 'Madonna look' by using different sizes of funnels.

October 18: Hid in a clothing rack and when people browsed through, yelled, 'PICK ME! PICK ME!'

October 21: When an announcement came over the loud speaker, he assumed a fetal position and screamed, 'OH NO! It's those voices again!'

And last, but not least:

October 23: Went into a fitting room, shut the door, waited awhile, and then yelled very loudly, 'Hey! There's no toilet paper in here.' One of the clerks passed out.

Is Golf like Marriage?

Golf can best be defined as an endless series of tragedies obscured by the occasional miracle, followed by a good beverage.

Golf! You hit down to make the ball go up. You swing left and the ball goes right. The lowest score wins. And on top of that, the winner buys the drinks.

Golf is harder than baseball. In golf, you have to play your foul balls.

If you find you do not mind playing golf in the rain, the snow, even during a hurricane, here's a valuable tip: your life is in trouble.

Golfers who try to make everything perfect before taking the shot rarely make a perfect shot.

A 'gimme' can best be defined as an agreement between two golfers...neither of whom can putt very well.

An interesting thing about golf is that no matter how badly you play, it is always possible to get worse.

Golf's a hard game to figure. One day you'll go out and slice it and shank it, hit into all the traps and miss every green. The next day you go out and for no reason at all you really stink.

If your best shots are the practice swings and the 'gimme putts,' you might wish to reconsider this game.

Golf is the only sport where the most feared opponent is you.

Golf is like marriage: if you take yourself too seriously it won't work, and both are expensive.

The best wood in most amateurs' bags is the pencil.

Anybody can be a Golfer

Pen & ink on 8x10 drawing paper

© 2011 Rafi

Why Golf Is Better Than Sex

#10. A below par performance is considered damn good.

#9. You can stop in the middle and have a cheeseburger and a couple of beers.

#8. It's much easier to find the sweet spot.

#7. Foursomes are encouraged.

#6. You can still make money doing it as a senior.

#5. Three times a day is possible.

#4. Your partner doesn't hire a lawyer if you play with someone else.

#3. If you live in Florida, you can do it almost every day.

#2. You don't have to cuddle with your partner when you're finished.

#1. And the NUMBER ONE reason why golf is better than sex: When your equipment gets old you can replace it!

A wise man once said, "Every society is judged by how it treats its least fortunate among them. There's a lesson in this fictional story for all of us.

A "SHAY" DAY

At a fund-raising dinner for a school that serves children with learning disabilities, the father of one of the students delivered a speech that would never be forgotten by all who attended. After extolling the school and its dedicated staff, he said, "When not interfered with by outside influences, everything nature does is done with perfection. Yet my son, Shay, cannot learn things as other children do. He cannot understand things as other children do. Where is the natural order of things in my son?" The audience was stilled by the query.

The father continued, "I believe that when a child like Shay, who is mentally and physically disabled, comes into the world, an opportunity to realize true human nature presents itself, and it comes in the way other people treat that child." Then he told the following story:

Shay and I had walked past a park where some boys Shay knew were playing baseball. Shay asked, "Do you think they'll let me play?" I knew that most of the boys would not want someone like Shay on their team, but as a father I also understood that if my son were allowed to play, it would give him a much-needed

WORDS

sense of belonging and some confidence that he was accepted by others in spite of his handicaps. I approached one of the boys on the field and asked (not expecting much) if Shay could play? The boy looked around for guidance and then said, "We're losing by six runs and the game is in the eighth inning. I guess he can be on our team and we'll try to put him in to bat in the ninth inning."

Shay struggled over to the team's bench and, with a broad smile, put on a team shirt. I watched with a small tear in my eye and warmth in my heart. The boys saw my joy at my son being accepted.

In the bottom of the eighth inning, Shay's team scored a few runs but was still behind by three. In the top of the ninth inning, Shay put on a glove and played in the right field. Even though no hits came his way, he was obviously ecstatic just to be in the game and on the field, grinning from ear to ear as I waved to him from the stands.

In the bottom of the ninth inning, Shay's team scored again. Now, with two outs and the bases loaded, the potential winning run was on base and Shay was scheduled to be next at bat. At this juncture, do they let Shay bat and give away their chance to win the game? Surprisingly, Shay was given the bat. Everyone knew that a hit was all but impossible because Shay didn't even know how to hold the bat properly, much less connect with the ball. However,

as Shay stepped up to the plate, the pitcher, recognizing that the other team was putting winning aside for this moment in Shay's life, moved in a few steps to lob the ball in softly so Shay could at least make contact.

The first pitch came and Shay swung clumsily and missed.

The pitcher again took a few steps forward to toss the ball softly towards Shay. As the pitch came in, Shay swung at the ball and hit a slow ground ball right back to the pitcher.

The game would now be over.

The pitcher picked up the soft grounder and could have easily thrown the ball to the first baseman. Shay would have been out and that would have been the end of the game. Instead, the pitcher threw the ball right over the first baseman's head, out of reach of all team mates.

Everyone from the stands and both teams started yelling, "Shay, run to first! Run to first!" Never in his life had Shay ever run that far, but he made it to first base. He scampered down the baseline, wide-eyed and startled. Everyone yelled, "Run to second, run to second!" Catching his breath, Shay awkwardly ran towards second, gleaming and struggling to make it to the base. By the time Shay rounded towards second base, the right fielder had the ball. The smallest guy on their team now had his first chance to be the hero for his team.

He could have thrown the ball to the second baseman for the tag, but he understood the pitcher's intentions so he, too, intentionally threw the ball high and far over the third baseman's head. Shay ran toward third base deliriously as the runners ahead of him circled the bases toward home.

All were screaming, "Shay, Shay, Shay, all the Way Shay." Shay reached third base because the opposing shortstop ran to help him by turning him in the direction of third base, and shouted, "Run to third! Shay, run to third!" As Shay rounded third, the boys from both teams, and the spectators, were on their feet screaming, "Shay, run home! Run home!"

Shay ran to home, stepped on the plate, and was cheered as the hero who hit the grand slam and won the game for his team.

That day, said the father softly with tears now rolling down his face, the boys from both teams helped bring a piece of true love and humanity into this world. Shay didn't make it to another summer. He died that winter, having never forgotten being the hero and making me so happy and coming home and having his Mother tearfully embrace her little hero of the day!

Snopes credits Rabbi Paysach Krohn as the author of the original version of this story, titled "Perfection at the Plate," in Krohn's book, "Echoes of the Maggi," published in 1999. Revised many times, it continues to circulate around the internet.

Is This The Wisdom Of
A Mature Adult?

If you die, I think part of a best friend's job should be to immediately clear your computer history.

Nothing sucks more than that moment during an argument when you realize you're wrong.

I totally take back all those times I didn't want to nap.

There is great need for a "sarcasm" font on your computer.

How the hell are you supposed to fold a fitted sheet?

Was learning cursive writing really necessary?

MapQuest really needs to start their directions on # 5. I'm pretty sure I know how to get out of my neighborhood.

Obituaries would be a lot more interesting if they told you how the person died.

I can't remember the last time I wasn't at least "kind of tired."

Bad decisions make good stories.

You never know when it will strike, but there comes a moment when you know you just aren't going to do anything productive for the rest of the day.

Can we all just agree to ignore whatever comes after Blu Ray? I don't want to have to restart my collection...again.

I'm always slightly terrified when I exit out of Word and it asks me if I want to save any changes to my 10-page technical report that I swear I did not make any changes to.

"Do not machine wash or tumble dry" means I will never wash this ever.

I hate when I just miss a call by the last ring ("Hello? Hello?") But when I immediately call back, it rings nine times and then goes to voice mail. What did you do after I didn't answer? Drop the phone and run away?

I hate leaving my house confident and looking good and then not seeing anyone of importance the entire day. What a waste.

I keep some people's phone numbers in my phone just so I know not to answer when they call.

WORDS

I think the freezer deserves a light as well.

I disagree with Kay Jewelers. I would bet on any given Friday or Saturday night more kisses begin with Miller Lite than Kay.

I wish Google Maps had an "Avoid Ghetto" routing option.

Sometimes, I'll watch a movie that I watched when I was younger and suddenly realize I had no idea what the heck was going on when I first saw it.

I would rather try to carry 10 overloaded plastic bags in each hand than take two trips to bring my groceries in.

The only time I look forward to a red light is when I'm trying to finish a text.

I have a hard time deciphering the fine line between boredom and hunger.

How many times is it appropriate to say, "What?" before you just nod and smile because you still didn't hear or understand a word they said?

I love the sense of camaraderie when an entire line of cars team up to prevent a jerk from cutting in at the front. Stay strong, brothers and sisters!

Shirts get dirty. Underwear gets dirty. Pants? Pants never get dirty, and you can wear them forever.

Is it just me, or do high school kids get dumber and dumber every year?

There's no worse feeling than that millisecond you're sure you are going to die after leaning your chair back a little too far.

As a driver I hate pedestrians, and as a pedestrian I hate drivers. But no matter what the mode of transportation, I always hate bicyclists.

Whoever wrote this has been through the mill! They deserve a prize.

This Is Why We Love Children!

Nudity

A little boy got lost at the YMCA and found himself in the women's locker room. When he was spotted, the room burst into shrieks, with ladies grabbing towels and running for cover. The little boy watched in amazement and then asked, "What's the matter, haven't you ever seen a little boy before?"

Opinions

On the first day of school, a first-grader handed his teacher a note from his mother. The note read, "The opinions expressed by this child are not necessarily those of his parents."

Ketchup

A woman was trying hard to get the ketchup out of the jar. During her struggle the phone rang so she asked her 4-year-old daughter to answer the phone. "Mommy can't come to the phone to talk to you right now. She's hitting the bottle."

Police

While taking a routine vandalism report at an elementary school, I was interrupted by a little girl about 6 years old. Looking up and down at my uniform, she asked, "Are you a cop?"

"Yes," I answered and continued writing the report.

"My mother said if I ever needed help I should ask the police. Is that right?"

"Yes, that's right," I told her.

"Well, then," she said as she extended her foot toward me, "would you please tie my shoe?"

Elderly

While working for an organization that delivers lunches to elderly shut-ins, I took my 4-year-old daughter on my afternoon rounds. She was unfailingly intrigued by the various appliances of old age, particularly the canes, walkers and wheelchairs. One day I found her staring at a pair of false teeth soaking in a glass. As I braced myself for the inevitable barrage of questions, she merely turned and whispered, "The tooth fairy will never believe this!"

WORDS

Dress Up

A little girl was watching her parents dress for a party. When she saw her dad donning his tuxedo, she warned, "Daddy, you shouldn't wear that suit."

"And why not, darling?"

"You know it always gives you a headache the next morning."

Death

While walking along the sidewalk in front of his church, our minister heard the intoning of a prayer that nearly made his collar wilt. Apparently, his 5-year-old son and his playmates had found a dead robin. Feeling that a proper burial should be performed, they had secured a small box and cotton batting, then dug a hole and made ready for the disposal of the deceased.

The minister's son was chosen to say the appropriate prayers. With sonorous dignity he intoned his version of what he thought his father always said: "Glory be to the Faaather, and unto the Sonnn, and into the hole he goooes."

Bible

A little boy opened the big family Bible. He was fascinated as he fingered through the old pages. Suddenly, something fell out of the Bible. He picked up the object and looked at it. What he saw was an old leaf that had been pressed in between the pages.

"Mama, look what I found," the boy called out.

"What have you got there, dear?"

With astonishment in the young boy's voice, he answered, "I think it's Adam's underwear!"

. . .just a few
special people

Thomas Jefferson

Graphite Stick on 8x10 drawing paper

© 2011 Rafi

Thomas Jefferson the Man

At 5, began studying under his cousin's tutor.

At 9, studied Latin, Greek and French.

At 14, studied classical literature and additional languages.

At 16, entered the College of William and Mary.

At 19, studied Law for 5 years, starting under George Wythe.

At 23, started his own law practice.

At 25, was elected to the Virginia House of Burgesses.

At 31, wrote the widely circulated "Summary View of the Rights of British America" and retired from his law practice.

At 32, was a Delegate to the Second Continental Congress.

At 33, wrote the Declaration of Independence.

At 33, took three years to revise Virginia's legal code, wrote a Public Education bill and a statute for Religious Freedom.

At 36, was elected the second Governor of Virginia, succeeding Patrick Henry.

At 40, served in Congress for two years.

At 41, was the American minister to France and negotiated commercial treaties with European nations along with Ben Franklin and John Adams.

At 46, served as the first Secretary of State under George Washington.

At 53, served as Vice President and was elected President of the American Philosophical Society.

At 55, drafted the Kentucky Resolutions and became the active head of the Republican Party.

At 57, was elected the third President of the United States.

At 60, obtained the Louisiana Purchase, doubling the nation's size.

At 60, was elected to a second term as President.

At 65, retired to Monticello.

At 80, helped President Monroe shape the Monroe Doctrine.

At 81, almost single-handedly created the University of Virginia and served as its first president.

At 83, died on the 50th anniversary of the Signing of the Declaration of Independence.

Thomas Jefferson knew about governance because he himself studied the previous failed attempts at government. He understood actual history, the nature of God, His laws and the nature of man. That happens to be way more than what most understand today. Jefferson really knew his stuff. He is a voice from the past to lead us in the future.

John F. Kennedy held a dinner in the white House for a group of the brightest minds in the nation at that time. He made this statement: "This is perhaps the assembly of the most intelligence ever to gather at one time in the White House, with the exception of when Thomas Jefferson dined alone."

Thomas Jefferson Said

When we get piled upon one another in large cities, as in Europe, we shall become as corrupt as Europe. ❧ The democracy will cease to exist when you take away from those who are willing to work and give to those who would not. ❧ It is incumbent on every generation to pay its own debts as it goes. A principle which, if acted on, would save one-half the wars of the world. ❧ I predict future happiness for Americans if they can prevent the government from wasting the labors of the people under the pretense of taking care of them. ❧ My reading of history convinces me that most bad government results from too much government. ❧ No free man shall ever be debarred the use of arms. ❧ The strongest reason for the people to retain the right to keep and bear arms is, as a last resort, to protect themselves against tyranny in government. ❧ The tree of liberty must be refreshed from time to time with the blood of patriots and tyrants. ❧ To compel a man to subsidize with his taxes the propagation of ideas which he disbelieves and abhors is sinful and tyrannical. ❧ I believe that banking institutions are more dangerous to our liberties than standing armies. If the American people ever allow private banks to control the issue of their currency, first by inflation, then by deflation, the banks and corporations that will grow up around the banks will deprive the people of all property until their children wake-up homeless on the continent their fathers conquered.

Last Real Cowboy

Graphite Stick on 18x24 Charcoal paper

© 2011 Rafi

These Folks Are Characters

Bigfoot Wallace, Deaf Smith, Gene Autry, Dale Evans, Bud Adams, Bum Phillips, Lyndon Johnson, Cactus Jack, Bayou Bob, San Antonio Rose, Dandy Don, Kinky Friedman, Pecos Bill, Judge Roy Bean, Spanky Mcfarland, Peppy Blount, Amarillo Slim, Chill Wills, Shanghai Pierce, Lightnin' Hopkins, Gatemouth Brown, Ma Ferguson, Ima Hogg, Texas Lil, Tex Ritter, Texas Guinan, Texas Jack Omohundro, Texas John Slaughter, Molly Ivins, Horney Toad Harley, Goose Tatum, Bear Bryant, Rip Torn, Peg Leg Ward, Clay Allison, Froggy Williams, Do Do Mcqueen, Bantam Ben Hogan, Barzillai Kuykendall, Mean Gene Greene, L. Q. Jones, Too Tall Jones, Spec Jackson, Pappy O'Daniel, Stovepipe Johnson, Cap'n Jack Hays, Cotton Plant Cotton, Flacco, Rip Ford, The Lone Ranger, Silver, Tonto, Scout, Froggy Williams, Night Train Lane, Mexico Thompson, Sissy Farenthold, Buddy Dial, Mean Joe Kelton, Cactus Pryor, Cotton Speyrer, Blackie Sherrod, Buck Owens, Wrong Way Corrigan, Spud Webb, Boomerang Billy, Willie Nelson, Babe Didrickson, Threelegged Willie, Whiskers Savage, Spade Cooley And Plano Joe

These folks are all characters. In any state where all those folks feel at home, you can be assured that state welcomes characters. That's Texas.

My friend, Tommy Feagins, sent me this little piece.

WORDS
TOGETHER IN
LOTS OF WAYS

Caveman and Rabbit

Pen & ink on 8x10 drawing paper

© 2011 Rafi

Imagine this fictional account taking place in the Stone Age during the Mesolithic period (roughly about 10,000 B.C) . It may have been a little later.

Caveman and Rabbit Stew

This story is about Doe, Ray and Mei, a hunter-gatherer family struggling to make it. At the beginning of the story, they're not.

The father, Ray, his wife, Doe, and their small son, Mei, are sitting around the evening camp fire, sharing the only food they have. The father had hunted all day, using his weapon, a big stick. He was only able to kill one small rabbit which they are now eating.

His words, translated into today's vernacular: "Honey, I'm sorry. I worked all day trying to get something for tonight's dinner, but was only able to get one rabbit. I saw a lot of them, but they were too fast for me."

"I know you tried, Ray," says Doe. "Look over there at Ugg's campfire. It looks like he only got one rabbit, too."

"Ummn, so he didn't do too well either," Ray says, scratching his beard. "I wonder. . . No. We don't work with others. Our family works alone. That's the way it's been forever... But, on the other hand, if Ugg and I stood at one end of the field and you and Ugg's wife and the kids drove the rabbits towards us, I'll bet we would get a better chance at hitting them. I think I'll talk to Ugg about it."

So, picking up the scrawny carcass of his rabbit, Ray slowly approaches Ugg's campfire. "Say, Ugg, got a minute? I want to talk to you about this idea I got today. I'd like your input."

Sure enough, the next hunt, using Ray's strategy of driving the rabbits towards him and Ugg, resulted in more rabbits for both families.

Born of necessity was an event that marked the beginning of cooperation between one man and another. It worked because each party to the transaction benefited. The wives and kids chased the rabbits in the field towards the two men who swung their clubs as fast and as furiously as they could. Together, both families got more rabbits than when working alone.

Imagine their conversation after they'd eaten their full.

"Say, Ugg," says Ray as he rubs his stomach. "Our hunt today went really well, don't you think?"

"Sure did," Ugg replies. "We got more today than I've ever gotten hunting alone. But there were a lot of rabbits we didn't get a chance to hit. I was thinking that if we chased them into that blind ravine, we might get a couple of chances at hitting them, once when they ran in and then again, when they ran out."

"That's a great idea," Ray says as he wanders back to his fire. "Let's try it tomorrow." He mumbles to himself, "That Ugg is not as dumb as he looks."

And thus these two ancients realized the benefits of two minds working together. It was a demonstration of innovation, of improving on an idea (plussing, as social observers say). Mankind moved up a notch.

The next day they doubled their kill. They appreciated the lesson of benefiting from the Spirit of Cooperation. Both benefited. They hunted like this for a long time, and their neighbors, seeing their success, started to hunt that way too.

Now the conversation around the night time fires was animated, as each hunter tried to outdo the others with stories of his successes.

One night, as Ray listened to the others, he was holding some twigs for the fire. He casually entwined them into a loose form, sort of like a net or fence. In a flash of inspiration, he thought to himself: "If I could make this longer and put it in front of the rabbits, then the rabbits that run by me would get caught in the sticks and I could hit them while they were struggling to get out."

For the next few weeks he experimented with his net. Finally, he was ready. He walked over to Ugg's camp, and, after the usual pleasantries were completed, said to Ugg, "Say, buddy, how would you like to double the number of rabbits you get each day?"

Ugg's eyes brightened. " That would be great. You know the little wife is going to have another baby and with the four I have to hunt for now, each day it gets harder and harder. Those teenagers eat like a brontosaurus. And another one on the way." To himself he mumbles, "I wonder what causes them?"

Ray explained his plan and showed Ugg the twig net.

Ray became a leader, revered because he knew how to do something Ugg did not. He was capable and could teach Ugg something, transferring a skill Ugg did not yet know how to do himself.

The next day the wives and kids were at one end of the field. They started walking towards their husbands, beating the grass and ground with their sticks and shouting. The rabbits started running away from them towards the net. The teenage sons held the net at each end and Ray and Ugg stood by, waiting for the rabbits to be snared. Their kill for the day was the biggest they had ever achieved. In fact, there were more rabbits than they could eat. Rather than let them spoil, they gave some away to their other neighbors.

And so Ray became known as the "Big Man," a guy who knew how to catch a lot of rabbits in a field. After a while, they shortened his title to "Chief."

A technological invention, the rabbit net, advanced civilization. Men were now able to provide more food than they needed, and thus had leftovers for others. They shared their catch, because they knew that if they gave some of their food away to those who had had a bad hunt day, they might get some food back on the day they, too, had a bad hunt.

A social event also occurred. A man emerged as a leader. He was a person who had a technical skill (how to make a rabbit net) and leadership knowledge (how to lead others so they would be able to get more rabbits).

By providing more food than was needed just to stay alive, competition among the neighbors was lessened, cooperation increased. They socialized more; they had more time to relax. And think.

One night someone said, "You know, we must have learned how to make pretty good coats from rabbit fur. I saw a guy the other day from one of the tribes over the hill, and he liked my coat. He had a stone axe I could really use. I wonder if he would trade me an axe for a rabbit coat?"

His wife spoke up, "I bet he would if I made my special collar for it. You know, the one you can pull up over your head when it gets really cold."

WORDS

Surplus food, creative thought, and travel resulted in commerce for profit. A technical advance. A teacher. A leader. An invention, a net for rabbits. Commerce, a rabbit coat for an axe. Civilization advanced another notch.

Throughout history, men have sought opportunity to, first of all, survive, and then, once survival needs were met, to improve his lot. Some have done a better job than others. Those who succeeded created a new range of opportunities for others.

How're you doing?

The Right Path

Pen & ink with wash on 8x10 drawing paper

© 2011 Rafi

WhereAreWeGoing?

Man has steadily progressed from the time of his creation. Today, when the guys get together, sooner or later they start speculating on "where will the future take us?" Although we may not see or understand, history is the answer. It points to the direction we are headed as plainly as if an arrow were shot from a bow towards a target so easy to hit it could not miss.

Granted, in the moments of time that history has been recorded, we have deviated from the path (the arrow seemed occasionally to have gone a long way from the direction the archer chose). But the Arrow of Destiny ultimately returns to its intended path and guides us towards the day we will achieve a global community of understanding. It would be a state we could call "heaven on earth." We're certainly not there yet.

Reconciling the creation of man and his transition from his primitive state to the man we know today has been and continues to be an object of thoughtful consideration for many people. What follows is a Christian explanation of this very evident path to the future. (The explanation may touch on examples of group dynamics you never have considered.)

My guides in this article have been Robert Wright, author of many books, but principally *"The Moral Animal"* and *"Nonzero,"* and Robert Axelrod's *"The Evolution of Cooperation."* Wright is a social anthropologist and student of Darwin. Axelrod is Professor of Political Science and Public Policy at the University of Michigan.

I have no trouble believing that God created man and woman, both who continue to grow closer to the angels. Man's intellect has been repeatedly successfully challenged and sharpened. His abilities have been and continue to be stressed and developed through challenge and response. The result has not always been what we would have liked, but history accepted the errors and made meaningful corrections in direction, like the arrow.

Man has always been faced with issues which required greater understanding, and, occasionally, uncommon responses. When faced with a challenge, man sometimes chooses answers that are "win win." But throughout history there are examples where man has ignored his understanding of what is best for all and chose a more selfish response.

Man has had the opportunity to make decisions that worked to the mutual advantage of his neighbors. When he did not, good results seldom occurred. But when he did, mankind progressed.

But making choices foreign to his existing social background were extreme challenges to intellect, but doable. Here are examples of how these choices might have occurred, based on Robert Wright's thinking.

Let's start with the premise that in a difficult situation where more than one person is involved, it is preferable for both parties to feel that the result was beneficial to them. For example, buying a car: if the car buyer feels he got a good deal, he's happy. And if the salesman feels the company got a good deal, he's happy. Unless both feel this way, a deal won't be made. It's the same way when a woman goes shopping and leaves her husband at home watching TV. Both are happy. Both feel they got the best solution possible.

In game theory this concept is called a "non-zero sum" event. In other words, the final score was zero to zero. Nobody lost; nobody won.

Getting to this point must have been extremely difficult for primitive man. Even modern man stumbles quite often. For example, Israel and Palestine are having trouble coming up with a solution that benefits both countries and results in a "win-win" for both.

How does the process that leads to cooperative change, a "win-win" solution, occur? It is a paradox.

Robert Alexrod's book, *The Evolution of Cooperation,* describes the prisoner's dilemma, a classic example of the value of cooperation. It goes like this:

Two partners in crime are being interrogated separately. There is not enough evidence to convict them of the crime they committed, but there is enough evidence to convict both of a lesser crime. This lesser crime would bring each a prison term of, say, one year. But the prosecutor wants a conviction on the more serious charge. Each man is pressured to confess and implicate the other.

The prosecutor says, "If you confess but your partner doesn't, I'll let you off free and use your testimony to lock him up for 10 years. And if you don't confess, yet your partner does, you go to prison for 10 years. If you confess and your partner does too, I'll put you both away, but only for three years."

The question is, "Will the two prisoners cooperate with each other according to their earlier agreement to refuse to confess? Or will one or both "defect" (cheat) and incriminate the other?" What each does is determined by two factors, **communication** and **trust.**

As strange as it seems, this same logic has guided us throughout history. "Can two nations cooperate and arrive at a conclusion that benefits both?"

The Prisoners' Options

Remain silent and so does your partner. The DA hasn't told you, but you'll only be put away for a year.

Cheat on your partner and confess. You're guaranteed not more than three years in prison, and you'll go free if your partner remains silent.

Remain silent. If your partner doesn't do the same, you're in the pokey for 10 years. The logic seems irresistible: don't cooperate with your partner, cheat on him. However, if both partners follow that logic, and both cheat, then both get three years in jail. If both stayed silent, each would have gotten just one year in jail.

So, both being mum is, relatively speaking, the win-win outcome. But it makes no sense for either partner to stay mum, unless both had been assured by the other that he will stay mum, too. That's why the first condition, "communication," is vital.

Axelrod's book delves into the many options and outcomes, including the creation of mathematical formulas which enable a computerized response to each option. It's complicated and the book is a difficult read. However, Axelrod sums things up by laying out four "simple suggestions" for positive outcomes that apply to prisoners, citizens and nations:

1. Don't be envious
2. Don't be the first to defect
3. Reciprocate both cooperation and defection
4. Don't be too clever.

He makes the case for promoting cooperating by suggesting that:
- The future is more important than the present.
- The payoff for cooperation should be greater than non-cooperation.
- Insuring that everyone knows the values, facts and skills that will promote cooperation.

Now, if we can just get world leaders to decide that cooperating would be better for everyone.

Another explanation of the four "simple suggestions' for positive outcomes is found in the article, "Your Style," in the first section of this book.

Whiskey Speech

Pencil drawing on 8x10 drawing paper

© 2011 Rafi

THE "WHISKEY SPEECH"

If you were educated in the South in the 50s, you'll remember it was a time when liquor "by the drink" was banned in most states. The argument, "dry" or "wet," was on the ballot in most county elections. One of the craftiest orations in the history of American politics was the "Whiskey Speech," delivered in April 1952 by young Mississippi legislator Noah S. "Soggy" Sweat, Jr.

My friends, I had not intended to discuss this controversial subject at this particular time. However, I want you to know that I do not shun controversy. On the contrary, I will take a stand on any issue at any time, regardless of how fraught with controversy it might be. You have asked me how I feel about whiskey. All right, here is how I feel about whiskey.

If, when you say "whiskey," you mean the devil's brew, the poisonous scourge, the bloody monster, the drink that defiles innocence, dethrones reason, destroys the home, creates misery and poverty, yea, literally takes the bread from the mouths of little children; if you mean the evil drink that topples the Christian man and woman from the pinnacle of righteous, gracious living into the bottomless pit of degradation and despair and shame and helplessness and hopelessness, then certainly I am against it.

But if, *when you say "whiskey," you mean the oil of conversation, the philosophic wine, the ale that is consumed when good fellows get together, that puts a song in their hearts and laughter on their lips, and the warm glow of contentment in their eyes; if you mean Christmas cheer; if you mean the stimulating drink that puts the spring in the old gentleman's step on a frosty, crispy morning; if you mean the drink which enables a man to magnify his joy and his happiness, and to forget, if only for a little while, life's great tragedies, and heartaches, and sorrows; if you mean that drink, the sale of which pours into our treasuries untold millions of dollars which are used to provide tender care for our little crippled children, our blind, our deaf, our dumb, our pitiful aged and infirm, to build highways and hospitals and schools, then certainly I am for it.*

This is my stand. I will not retreat from it. I will not compromise.

Following are the words of Madame Lily Bollinger (1899-1976, writing in "Champagne Bollinger," on the subject of Champagne:

I drink it when I'm happy and when I'm sad.
Sometimes I drink it when I'm alone.
When I have company, I consider it obligatory.
I trifle with it if I'm not hungry and drink it when I am.
Otherwise I never touch the stuff...unless I'm thirsty."

WORDS

Consonants and Vowels

Put them together and they become words.

There are words...and then there are words. When words, phrases or sentences are used frequently or mistakenly, they sometimes get "named." Intentionally or accidentally, words say something to the listener or reader that is meaningful, serious, funny, winsome, romantic, frightening, or nonsensical. The intellectual challenge is combining them properly.

In the pages that follow are definitions and illustrations of many of the most popular combinations—all of which you want to have at the tip of your tongue. There are examples of the more familiar word combinations and fewer examples of the lesser-known (and less frequently used ones.) Some won't be mentioned at all. So, if you want more information than is in this article, go to Google, or funwithwords. com, or acronymfinder.com or your favorite reference source. They are the sources I used.

"Consonants and Vowels" is for anyone who wonders, "What do I say now?" or "Why did I say that?"

First, a fast introduction to the more popular combinations and, then, on subsequent pages, examples:

An **Acronym** is an abbreviation formed from the initial letters of a series of words. Two examples: NATO (for the North Atlantic Treaty Organization) or NASA (for the National Aeronautics and Space Administration).

An **Anagram** is a word, phrase, or sentence formed from another by rearranging its letters. For example, "Angel" is an anagram of "glean."

A **Cliché** is an expression, idea, or element of an artistic work which has been overused to the point of losing its original meaning or effect, rendering it a stereotype.

A **Euphemism** is the substitution of a mild, indirect, or vague expression for an expression thought to be offensive, harsh, or blunt. For example, the expression, "To pass away" is a euphemism for "to die."

A **Malapropism** is used to describe those verbal slips and gaffs we all have made—any sentence where one word is incorrectly used in place of another. A good example is "He's a wolf in cheap clothing." Some more recent malapropisms are know as Bushisms.

A **Metaphor** is a figure of speech in which an expression is used to refer to something that it does not literally denote in order to suggest a similarity, as in *"love is a battlefield."*

A **Mondegreen** results from something mis-heard rather than mis-said.

An **Oxymoron** is a phrase in which two words of contradictory meaning are used together for special effect, e.g. *"wise fool," "legal murder," "new-classic;" "positive-aggression;" or "peace-force."*

A **Palindrome** is a word, phrase, verse, or sentence that reads the same backward or forward. For example: "A man, a plan, a canal, Panama." (Think about it; it works.)

A **Pangram** uses every letter of the alphabet at least once in a sentence. Everybody knows one or two pangrams, *"The quick brown fox jumps over a lazy dog,"* or *"Pack my box with five dozen liquor jugs."*

A **Pleonasm** is the use of more words than are necessary to express an idea. Most often, some of the words are redundant. For example, *"a free gift "or true fact.*

A **Paraprosdokian** is a figure of speech in which the latter part of a sentence or phrase is surprising or unexpected in a way that causes the reader or listener to reframe or reinterpret the first part.

Spoonerisms (my favorite) are words or phrases in which letters or syllables get swapped. This often happens accidentally in slips of the tongue (or *"tips of the slung!"*).

Following are examples of the definitions cited above. They have been intentionally edited enough that you will see illustrations, but not too many.

Fave hun!

Ac•ro•nym

An **Acronym** is an abbreviation formed from the initial letters of a series of words.

Shown below is a small section of the 312 listings the web site acronymfinder.com shows for the acronym, "ACE." The web site says there are 250 more ACE acronyms in their sister compilation, "Acronym Attic."

There are sub-sections within the 312 ACE acronyms.

It seems there's an acronym for everything. If you want to be **really** impressed, go to the web site and look at the whole list.

ACRONYMS for "ACE" *(A partial list)*

Aviation Combat Element (MAGTF)

Automatic Content Extraction

Automatic Computing Engine

Agricultural Communicators in Education

Arts Council of England

Aviation Combat Element

Attempt to Controlled English (linguistics)

Australian Computer Society

ASCII Compatible Encoding

Analysis and Control Element

Annual Conference and Exposition

Alternatives for Community and Environment

Association of Consulting Engineers

Assured Computing Environment

American Cultural Exchange

An•a•gram

An **Anagram** is a word, phrase, or sentence formed from another by re-arranging its letters. Some examples:

Desperation = A rope ends it

Eleven plus two = Twelve plus one

Fingertips = Finest grip

Fir cones = Conifers

Flamethrower = Oh, felt warmer

Funeral = Real fun

Garbage Man = Bag Manager

Geologist = Go Get Oils

George Bush = He bugs Gore

Hot water = Worth tea

I hate school = Oh so ethical

I run to escape = A persecution

I spared = A spider

Indomitableness = Endless ambition

Jay Leno = Enjoy LA

Jennifer Aniston = Fine in torn jeans

Justin Timberlake = I'm a jerk but listen

Ladybug = Bald guy

Laxative = Exit lava

Listen = Silent

Madam Curie = Radium came

Margaret Thatcher = That great charmer

Meal for one = For me alone

Narcissism = Man's crisis

Ap•o•si•o•pe•sis

Aposiopesis is a rhetorical term wherein a sentence is deliberately broken off and left unfinished, the ending to be supplied by the imagination. Aposiopesis can simulate the impression of a speaker so overwhelmed by emotions that he or she is unable to continue speaking. It can also convey a certain pretended shyness toward obscene expressions or even an everyday casualness. The word is from the Greek, "maintaining silence." *Explanation by Richard Nordquist and Andrea Grun-Oesterreich. Examples are from literature and TV.*

Examples:

"Just because you own half the county doesn't mean that you have the power to run the rest of us. For 23 years I've been dying to tell you what I thought of you! And now...well, being a Christian woman, I can't say it!"
(Auntie Emin, The Wizard of Oz, 1939)

"I will have such revenges on you both
"That all the world shall know I will do things. . .
"What they are yet, I know not;
"but they shall be the terrors of the earth!"
(William Shakespeare, King Lear)

"I won't sleep in the same bed with a woman who thinks I'm lazy! I'm going right downstairs, unfold the couch, unroll the sleeping bag... uh, goodnight."
(Homer Simpson in The Simpsons)

"Dear Ketel One Drinker--There comes a time in everyone's life when they just want to stop what they're doing and ... .
(Print ad for Ketel One vodka, 2007)

Cli•chés

A **Cliché** is an expression, idea, or element of an artistic work which has been overused to the point of losing its original meaning or effect, rendering it a stereotype, especially when at some earlier time it was considered meaningful or novel.

The term, according to Wikipedia, is frequently used in modern culture for an action or idea which is expected or predictable, based on a prior event. Typically, "clichés" express criticism or disapproval; and while they are not always false or inaccurate, a cliché may or may not be true. Some are stereotypes, but some are simply truisms and facts. Clichés are often for comic effect, typically in fiction. You know... know what I mean?

According to Wikipedia, using clichés in writing or speech is generally considered a mark of inexperience or unoriginality. What follows are just a few examples of clichés. There are thousands. Google "cliché˝" if you have a compulsion to know more trite expressions.

Animals
"A hair of the dog that bit you" (meaning the idea that a small part of the thing that harmed you will now help you. Specifically, having a drink in the morning when you have a hangover).

Food and Drink
"A spoon full of sugar helps the medicine go down" (meaning a little bit of something nice makes it easier to handle something bad).

Money
"A fool and his money are soon parted" (meaning behaving foolishly with money will result in losing it or being tricked out of it).
"Give him a run for his money."
"Making money hand over fist."
"Money burns a hole in his pocket."
"Money is the root of all evil."
"In the money."
"Money makes the world go round."
"He's got more money than he knows what to do with."

General Clichés
"A little of this, a little of that" (meaning a mélange of several things). For example:
"What did you have for dinner?"
"Oh, a little of this, a little of that."
"In other words, some of everything."
"Yeah."

Some more clichés using the word, "little:"

"*A little yeast works through the whole batch of dough.*"
"*Don't use a lot where a little will do.*"
"*Give a little, take a little.*"
"*I'll fix your little red wagon.*"
"*Into every life a little rain must fall.*"
"*My little black book.*"
"*Put a little elbow grease in to it.*"
"*So many men, so little time.*"

Modern day language is filled with clichés. Check the web if you want to expand your vocabulary with phrases that have been honed to perfection by unimaginative people.

Eu•phe•mism

A **Euphemism** is the substitution of a mild, indirect, or vague expression for one thought to be offensive, harsh, or blunt.

"**Euphemisms** are not, as many young people think, useless verbiage for that which can and should be said bluntly; they are like secret agents on a delicate mission, they must airily pass by a stinking mess with barely so much as a nod of the head. Euphemisms are unpleasant truths wearing diplomatic cologne." *(Quentin Crisp, Manners from Heaven, 1984)*

Euphemisms are commonly used in everyday conversation and may well be the most used of all word combinations. For example, "Crazy" originally meant 'cracked, flawed, damaged' and was applicable to all manner of illness; but it has now narrowed to refer to 'mental illness.'

'Crazy' refers to the stereotypical mental patient as someone 'flawed or deficient,' and is the basis for many **euphemistic** expressions for madness: *crack-brained, scatterbrained; head case, nutcase, bonkers, wacko, wacky; falling to pieces; have a nervous breakdown; unhinged; having a screw loose; one brick short of a load; not a full load; not playing with a full deck; three cards short of a full deck; one sandwich short of a picnic; his elevator doesn't go to the top floor; a shingle short; he's lost his marbles."*
(Keith Allen and Kate Burridge, Euphemism and Dysphemism: Language Used as a Shield and Weapon. Oxford Univ. Press, 1991)

See what I mean?

Following are a few euphemism examples; you'll easily figure out the phrase they replace.

Adult Entertainment	Eternal Rest
Ample Proportions	Expecting
Armed Intervention	Fabricate
Au Natural	Fall Asleep
Be Excused	Friendly Fire
Between Jobs	Full Figured
Big Boned	Gentleman Friend
Bit the Big One	In An Interesting Condition
Bitten the Dust	In Reduced Circumstances
Cash In Your Chips	Indisposed
Cement Shoes	Kick the Bucket
Departed	Knocked Up
Direct mail	Lady of the Night
Disinformation	Laid Off
Electronic Surveillance	Landfill

WORDS

Mal•a•prop•isms

Malapropisms are verbal slips and gaffes. The word means any sentence in which one word has been used incorrectly in place of another, either due to ignorance or a temporary slip of the tongue.

Author Richard Sheridan introduced a humorous character named Mrs. Malaprop in his 1775 Restoration comedy, "The Rivals." Mrs. Malaprop substituted similar-sounding words for the words she actually intended to use. The consequence was a hilariously nonsensical sentence now referred to as a "Malapropism."

Here are a handful of malapropisms gathered by *fun-withwords.com:*

He had to use a fire distinguisher.

Dad says the monster is just a pigment of my imagination.

Isn't that an expensive pendulum round that man's neck?

Good punctuation means not to be late.

He's a wolf in cheap clothing.

Michelangelo painted the Sixteenth Chapel.

My sister has extra-century perception.

"Don't" is a contraption.

Flying saucers are just an optical conclusion.

A rolling stone gathers no moths.

Bush•isms

President George W. Bush is famous for his malapropisms, so much so that malapropisms are often referred to as "Bushisms." Here are a few choice Bushisms:

"Oftentimes, we live in a processed world, you know, people focus on the process and not results."

"It will take time to restore chaos and order."

"We need an energy bill that encourages consumption."

"We are making steadfast progress."

Met•a•phor

A **metaphor** is a figure of speech in which an expression is used to refer to something that it does not literally denote in order to suggest a similarity. A metaphor shows how two things that are not alike in most ways are similar in one important way.

There are so many metaphors used in everyday communications that web pages which show illustrations of metaphors have categorized them generally as:

War Metaphors	Fishing Metaphors
Family Metaphors	Farming Metaphors
Weather Metaphors	Sensory Metaphors
Cooking Metaphors	

Here is a grouping of Weather Metaphors *(explanations are shown within the parenthesis):*

Autumn: They had entered their autumn years *(one's life is a single year).*

Blizzard: There was a blizzard of activity at the emergency room *(seemingly erratic movement).*

Blow: You'll be blown away! *(our position is susceptible to sudden change).*

Breeze: This home work is a breeze *(challenge is an opposing force).*

Chilly: It's been a little chilly around the office since Mr. Iron Britches became boss! *(an office has an emotional climate, which may be invaded by a cold front).*

Clear skies: It's gonna' be clear skies from now on *(clear skies are not a threat).*

Cloud: The event was clouded over by protests *(protests are an intrusion of light).*

Cold: A cold reception *(a gathering has a climate).*

Darken: The skies of his future began to darken *(darkness is a threat).*

Dawn: The dawn of civilization *(civilization has its day).*

Drift: He was a drifter, of origin unknown *(a lack of will is a lack of destination).*

Dry spell: Business suffered a long dry spell *(revenue is the welcome rain of business).*

Fog: My memory is a little foggy *(memory is a visible object).*

Grey skies: Grey skies are gonna' clear up! *(rain is bad).*

Gust: Criticism began to gust in from all sides *(critics are blow hards!).*

Hail: A hail of bullets *(cold, hard and driven).*

WORDS

Lightening rod: He became a lightning rod for party criticism *(criticism is negative energy from above)*.

Misty: Misty, water-colored memories *(memories are neither solid nor distinct)*.

Rain: Into each life some rain must fall *(hardship is a precipitate from above)*.

Season: It is the season of change *(change is natural, occurring in phases, spaced by a lack of change)*.

Storm: She was unsure if her proposal could weather the storm of scrutiny *(scrutiny is harsh weather to one's ideas)*.

Sunset: He'd entered his sunset years *(one's life is a single day)*.

Sunshine: You are the sunshine of my life *(happiness is light)*.

Thaw: Relations between the two countries began to thaw *(relationships can be frozen solid, making change or growth impossible)*.

Thunder: The boss thundered into the room *(anger is hostile weather)*.

Weather: His face was weathered by a long, troubled life *(bad events wear the youth from our face)*.

Whirlwind: It was a whirlwind romance that spun out of control *(romance may be phenomenal and brief)*.

Wind: The winds of change *(change is the product of lateral forces)*.

Google "metaphor" for more examples.

Mon•de•greens

Mondegreens are, in a sense, the opposite of malapropisms; they result from something being mis-heard rather than mis-said. Here are a few misheard song lyrics, followed by the correct words:

"Excuse me while I kiss this guy."
"Excuse me while I kiss the sky."
Purple Haze, Jimi Hendrix

"There's a bathroom on the right."
"There's a bad moon on the rise."
Bad Moon Rising, Creedence Clearwater Revival

"The girl with colitis goes by."
"The girl with kaleidoscope eyes."
Lucy in the Sky with Diamonds, The Beatles

"Crimean River."
"Cry Me a River."
Cry Me a River, Julie London

WORDS

Ox•y•mo•rons

An **Oxymoron** is a figure of speech that uses seeming contradictions. There are a lot of them; here are a few:

12-ounce pound-cake
Act natural
California culture
Clearly misunderstood
Computer jock
Definite maybe
Diet ice cream
Exact estimate
First annual
Found missing
Fresh frozen
Genuine imitation
Good grief
Mild abrasive
Military intelligence
Minor disaster
New classic
Now then
Organized mess

Original copy
Passive aggressive
Peace force
Plastic glasses
Political science
Pretty ugly
Rap music
Second best
Small crowd
Software documentation
Student teacher
Sure bet
Sweet sorrow
Synthetic natural gas
Taped live
Temporary tax increase
Terribly pleased
Tight slacks
Working vacation

Pal•in•drome

A **Palindrome** is a word, phrase, verse, or sentence that reads the same backward or forward.

Palindrome Names
Ana
Elle
Eve
Hannah
Zerimar Ramirez (an actual person)

Palindrome Phrases
A but tuba.
A car, a man, a maraca.
A dog, a plan, a canal: pagoda.
A dog! A panic in a pagoda!
A lad named E. Mandala
A man, a plan, a canal: Panama.
A nut for a jar of tuna.
A Santa at Nasa.
A Toyota! Race fast, safe car! A Toyota!
Avid diva.
Baby Bab
Bar an arab
Bird rib.
Borrow or rob?
Camp Mac
Campus motto: Bottoms up Mac.

Palindrome Words

aibohphobia	dewed	noon	rotor
alula	evitative	party-trap	sexes
boob	kayak	racecar	solos
cammac	lemel	radar	space caps
civic	level	refer	stats
deified	madam	repaper	tenet
deleveled	mom	rotator	

W O R D S

Pan•gram

A **Pangram** uses every letter of the alphabet at least once. Pangramists have long sought the perfect pangram, a 26-letter sentence containing every letter of the alphabet exactly once, with varying success. One of the best known is: **Mr. Jock, TV quiz PhD, bags few lynx.**

Here are some more pangrams, all which use every letter of the alphabet at least once.

The five boxing wizards jump quickly.

Sympathizing would fix Quaker objectives.

Many-wived Jack laughs at probes of sex quiz.

Turgid saxophones blew over Mick's jazzy quaff.

Playing jazz vibe chords quickly excites my wife.

A large fawn jumped quickly over white zinc boxes.

Exquisite farm wench gives body jolt to prize stinker.

Jack amazed a few girls by dropping the antique onyx vase!

The quick brown fox jumps over a lazy dog.

Pack my box with five dozen liquor jugs.

Para•pros•do•kian

A **Paraprosdokian** is a figure of speech in which the latter part of a sentence or phrase is surprising or unexpected in a way that causes the reader or listener to reframe or reinterpret the first part. Some examples:

Do not argue with an idiot. He will drag you down to his level and beat you with experience.

I want to die peacefully in my sleep, like my grandfather. Not screaming and yelling like the passengers in his car.

Going to church doesn't make you a Christian any more than standing in a garage makes you a car.

Light travels faster than sound. This is why some people appear bright until you hear them speak.

If I agreed with you we'd both be wrong.

We never really grow up; we only learn how to act in public.

War does not determine who is right - only who is left.

Knowledge knows a tomato is a fruit; wisdom is not putting it in a fruit salad.

The early bird might get the worm, but the second mouse gets the cheese.

Evening news is where they begin with "Good evening," and then proceed to tell you why it isn't.

To steal ideas from one person is plagiarism. To steal from many is research.

A bus station is where a bus stops. A train station is where a train stops. On my desk, I have a work station.

How it is one careless match can start a forest fire, but it takes a whole box to start a campfire?

I used to be indecisive. Now I'm not sure.

Dolphins are so smart that within a few weeks of captivity, they can train people to stand on the very edge of the pool and throw them fish.

I didn't say it was your fault, I said I was blaming you.

Women will never be equal to men until they can walk down the street with a bald head and a beer gut and still think they are sexy.

Why do Americans choose from just two people to run for president and 50 for Miss America?

Behind every successful man is his woman. Behind the fall of a successful man is usually another woman.

A clear conscience is usually the sign of a bad memory.

You do not need a parachute to skydive. You only need a parachute to skydive twice.

The voices in my head may not be real, but they have some good ideas!

Always borrow money from a pessimist. He won't expect it back.

Nostalgia isn't what it used to be.

Money can't buy happiness, but it sure makes misery easier to live with.

Some cause happiness wherever they go. Others whenever they go.

I always take life with a grain of salt, plus a slice of lemon and a shot of tequila.

When tempted to fight fire with fire, remember that the Fire Department usually uses water.

You're never too old to learn something stupid.

To be sure of hitting the target, shoot first and call whatever you hit the target.

Ple•o•nasms

A **Pleonasm** is the use of more words than are necessary to express an idea; consequently, some of the words are redundant. For example, *a free gift or true fact*. A few examples of pleonasms are shown below.

Google pleonasm to see lots more.

A.M. in the morning
absolutely necessary
added bonus
advance planning
all-time record
alternative choice
anonymous stranger
armed gunman
artificial prosthesis
assemble together
autobiography of his or her own life
bald-headed

basic necessities
best ever
cooperate together
completely eliminate
completely surround
component parts
consensus of opinion
constantly maintained
current incumbent
depreciate in value
disappear from sight

WORDS

Phobia Words

Have you been afraid of something for a long, long time? Does the mention of a word or an object send chills up and down your spine? Do you sometimes wake up from a deep sleep in a cold sweat? You might have a **"phobia."**

Phobia comes from the Greek and means fear or hatred. Three commonly known phobias are **arachnophobia** (fear of spiders), **claustrophobia** (fear of confined spaces), and **agoraphobia** (fear of open spaces). There are phobia words for the fear of heights, snakes, flying, the sight of blood, fear of chickens, your stepmother, Chinese people, beards...
even giving birth to monsters!

However, not all phobia words mean fear or hatred. Sometimes the meaning is that of an intolerance or aversion to something. For example, **hypophobia** is not a fear or intolerance at all; it means an absence of fear. *Funwithwords.com* has gathered almost 650 phobia names, creating the largest ever list of such words. Following is a small sampling of the names of phobias that have been collected. Go to the web site for more.

ablutophobia - fear of bathing

acarophobia - fear of mites or itching

acerophobia - fear of sourness

achluophobia - fear of darkness

acidophobia - aversion (of plants to acidic soil)

acousticophobia - fear of noise

acrophobia - fear of heights

aeronausiphobia - fear of airplanes

aerophobia - fear of air and drafts

agoraphobia - fear of open spaces

agraphobia - fear of sexual abuse

agrizoophobia - fear of wild animals

Put Downs
(also known as "Smugopedia")

Slightly controversial opinions—put downs you can throw into a conversation—are called **"smugopedia"** by the developer of the smugopedia website, S. Morgan Friedman. He says using these putdowns offers you the chance to buy a fleeting sense of self-satisfaction at the small cost of alienating your friends and loved ones.

For example, a subject comes up that one of the crowd speaks on as an "expert," and you don't think they are...use a "Smugopedia" retort. Following are examples:

Luciano Pavarotti
"Although Pavarotti was clearly very talented, his fame was inflated by the London and Decca marketing machines. Domingo or even Corelli were obviously his equal."

King Lear
"Although King Lear is rivaled perhaps only by Hamlet, I tend to agree with critic Charles Lamb's observation that it ought to be read, not performed."

C. S. Lewis
"The original 1985 BBC movie about the life of C. S. Lewis, *Shadowlands,* is more subtly directed and nuanced than the 1993 movie. And unlike Anthony Hopkins, Joss Ackland actually looks like C. S. Lewis." *(Smug source: Dave Barnette)*

Sushi
"It's only worth bothering with sushi if you're going to go to the Tokyo Fish Market. Nothing else is really fresh enough to capture the perfect simplicity of toro or uni."

Bickering
"Departmental bickering always reminds me of Borges' observation on the Falklands War: It's like two bald men fighting over a comb."

WORDS

Spoon•er•isms

Spoonerisms are words or phrases in which letters or syllables get swapped. This often happens accidentally in slips of the tongue (or "tips of the slung" as Spoonerisms are often affectionately called!). The word spoonerism, comes from William Archibald Spooner who was famous for making verbal slips. Just look at these typical spoonerisms:

Tease my ears (Ease my tears)
A lack of pies (A pack of lies)
It's roaring with pain (It's pouring with rain)
Wave the sails (Save the whales)
Chipping the flannel (Flipping the channel)
In the lead of spite (In spite of the lead)
Go and shake a tower (Go and take a shower)
Cat flap (Flat cap)
Bad salad (Sad ballad)
Soap in your hole (Hope in your soul)
Mean as custard (Keen as mustard)
Plaster man (Master plan)
Pleating and humming (Heating and plumbing)
Birthington's washday (Washington's birthday)
Snail tracks (Trail snacks)
Bottle in front of me (Frontal lobotomy)
Sale of two titties (Tale of Two Cities)
Rental Deceptionist (Dental receptionist)
Flock of bats (Block of flats)
Chewing the doors (Doing the chores)

There're more! Following are spoonerized titles of popular fairy tales:

Prinderella and the Cince (Cinderella and the Prince)
Beeping Sleauty (Sleeping Beauty)
The Pea Little Thrigs (The Three Little Pigs)
Goldybear and the Three Locks (Goldilocks and the Three Bears)
Ali Theeva and the Forty Babs (Ali Baba and the Forty Thieves)

My favorite spoonerism stories:

Evidence has been found that William Tell and his family were avid bowlers. Unfortunately, all the Swiss league records were destroyed in a fire, so we'll never know for whom the Tells bowled.

King Ozymandias of Assyria was running low on cash after years of war with the Hittites. His last great possession was the Star of the Euphrates, the most valuable diamond in the ancient world. Desperate, he went to Croesus, the pawnbroker, to ask for a loan. Croesus said, "I'll give you 100,000 dinars for it."

"But I paid a million dinars for it," the King protested. "Don't you know who I am? I am the king!"

Croesus replied, "When you wish to pawn a Star, makes no difference who you are."

A man rushed into a busy doctor's office and shouted, "Doctor! I think I'm shrinking!"

The doctor calmly responded, "Now, now. Settle down. You'll just have to be a little patient."

Back in the 1800's the Tate's Watch Company of Massachusetts wanted to produce other products, and since they already made the cases for watches, they used them to produce compasses. The new compasses were so bad that people often ended up in Canada or Mexico rather than California. This, of course, is the origin of the expression, "He who has a Tate is lost!"

A thief broke into the local police station and stole all the toilets and urinals, leaving no clues. A spokesperson was quoted as saying, "We have absolutely nothing to go on."

An Indian chief was feeling very sick, so he summoned the medicine man. After a brief examination, the medicine man took out a long, thin strip of elk rawhide and gave it to the chief, telling him to bite off, chew, and swallow one inch of the leather every day. After a month, the medicine man returned to see how the chief was feeling. The chief shrugged and said, "The thong is ended, but the malady lingers on."

A famous Viking explorer returned home from a voyage and found his name missing from the town register. His wife insisted on complaining to the local civic official who apologized profusely saying, "I must have taken Leif off my census."

A skeptical anthropologist was cataloging South American folk remedies with the assistance of a tribal Brujo who indicated that the leaves of a particular fern were a sure cure for any case of constipation. When the anthropologist expressed his doubts, the Brujo looked him in the eye and said, "Let me tell you, with fronds like these, you don't need enemas!"

Interesting Words Re-Defined

ADULT A person who has stopped growing at both ends and is now growing in the middle.

BEAUTY PARLOR A place where women curl up and dye.

CANNIBAL Someone who is fed up with people.

CHICKEN An animal you eat before they are born and after they are dead.

COMMITTEE A body that keeps minutes and wastes hours.

DUST Mud with the juice squeezed out.

EGOTIST Someone who is usually me-deep in conversation.

HANDKERCHIEF Cold Storage.

INFLATION Cutting money in half without damaging the paper.

MOSQUITO An insect that makes you like flies better.

SECRET Something you tell to one person at a time.

TOOTHACHE The pain that drives you to extraction.

TOMORROW One of the greatest labor saving devices of today.

YAWN An honest opinion openly expressed.

WRINKLES Something other people have, similar to your character lines.

Can You Read These Words Right?

The bandage was **wound** around the **wound**.

The farm was used to **produce produce** .

The dump was so full that it had to **refuse** more **refuse**.

We must **polish** the **Polish** furniture.

He could **lead** if he would get the **lead** out.

The soldier decided to **desert** his dessert in the **desert**.

Since there is no time like the **present**, he thought it was time to **present** the **present**.

A **bass** was painted on the head of the **bass** drum.

When shot at, the **dove dove** into the bushes.

I did not **object** to the **object**.

The insurance was **invalid** for the **invalid**.

There was a **row** among the oarsmen about how to **row**.

They were too **close** to the door to **close** it.

The buck **does** funny things when the **does** are present.

A seamstress and a **sewer** fell down into a **sewer** line.

To help with planting, the farmer taught his **sow** to **sow**.

The **wind** was too strong to **wind** the sail.

Upon seeing the **tear** in the painting I shed a **tear**.

I had to **subject** the **subject** to a series of tests.

How can I **intimate** this to my most **intimate** friend?

Let's face it, English is a crazy language. There is no egg in eggplant, nor ham in hamburger; neither apple nor pine in pineapple. English muffins weren't invented in England or French fries in France. Sweetmeats are candies while sweetbreads, which aren't sweet, are meat.

We take English for granted. But if we explore its paradoxes, we find that quicksand can work slowly, boxing rings are square and a guinea pig is neither from Guinea nor is it a pig. Ship by truck and send cargo by ship? Have noses that run and feet that smell? How can a slim chance and a fat chance be the same, while a wise man and a wise guy are opposites?

You have to marvel at the unique lunacy of a language in which your house can burn up as it burns down, in which you fill in a form by filling it out and in which an alarm goes off by going on.

English was invented by people, not computers, and it reflects the creativity of the human race, which, of course, is not a race at all. That is why, when the stars are out, they are visible, but when the lights are out, they are invisible.

P.S. -Why doesn't 'Buick' rhyme with 'quick?'

W O R D S

A Word For Lovers Of The English Language

There is a two-letter word that has more meanings than any other two-letter word, and that is UP.

It's easy to understand UP, meaning toward the sky or at the top of the list, but when we awaken in the morning, why do we wake UP? At a meeting, why does a topic come UP? Why do we speak UP and why are the officers UP for election and why is it UP to the secretary to write UP a report?

We call UP our friends. And we brighten UP a room, polish UP the silver; we warm UP the leftovers and clean UP the kitchen. We lock UP the house, and some guys fix UP the old car. At other times the little word has real special meaning. People stir UP trouble, line UP for tickets, work UP an appetite, and think UP excuses. To be dressed is one thing but to be dressed UP is special.

And this UP is confusing: A drain must be opened UP because it is stopped UP. We open UP a store in the morning, but we close it UP at night.

We seem to be pretty mixed UP about UP! To be knowledgeable about the proper uses of UP, look the word UP in the dictionary. In a desk-sized dictionary, it takes UP almost a quarter of the page and can add UP to about thirty definitions. If you are UP to it, you might try building UP a list of the many ways UP is used. It will take UP a lot of your time, but if you don't give UP, you may wind UP with a hundred or more.

When it threatens to rain, we say it is clouding UP. When the sun comes out, we say it is clearing UP.

When it rains, it wets the earth and often messes things UP. When it doesn't rain for a while, things dry UP.

One could go on and on, but I'll wrap it UP, for now my time is UP, so time to shut UP!

Oh, one more thing: What is the first thing you do in the morning and the last thing you do at night? U-P!

WORDS

JUST

FOR

YOU

Angel Dust

Pencil drawing on paper

© 2011 Rafi

The Best Way to Spend the Day

Can you spend the whole day loving people, demonstrating joy, peace, patience, kindness, generosity, faithfulness, gentleness, and self-control?

If you can, then you're enjoying the fruits of the spirit.

Galatians 5:22-23

Angels Can't Do Everything

Pen ank Ink on 8x10 drawing paper

© 2011 Rafi

The Learning Process, an Easy Example

There was a time when you **didn't know you didn't know how** to tie your shoes.

Then, one day **you discovered you didn't know how** to tie your shoes, and you wanted to.

You began trying, but failed. **Someone (like your Mother) instructed you and guided you** as you went through the motions.

You **learned how** to tie your shoes, but **did so only consciously.** You practiced.

You now **tie your shoes without giving the act a thought.**

You can now work on something else...like eliminating cancer. The same process works.

You've just gone through the process that continues to change the world.

Thanks.

NOTE: Since writing the shoe-tying piece I have learned about the work of Daniel Willingham, a psychologist at the University of Virginia. He differentiates between "explicit learning" and "implicit learning," the "technical" points of the previous article.

Being taught to tie your shoes is an example of **explicit** *learning. When you were first taught by your mother or someone else, you followed their instructions in a deliberate and mechanical manner.*

But as you learned the process and became more confident, the **implicit** *process took over. You would tie your shoes without thinking. In fact, I doubt that today you give the shoe-tying process a second thought. You just do it.*

Willingham makes another interesting observation: under periods of stress, you do not rely on the implicit (unthinking) process to dominate. Instead, you choke. Your explicit learning process takes over, along with all its requirements for concentration and deliberate movement. In a sense, you're a child again, waiting for your mother to tell you what to do next, and then trying your childish best to comply. There's no unconscious response. Incidentally, there's a big difference between "choking"—thinking too much—and "panicking"—thinking too little. But that's another story (one best told by Malcomb Gladwell).

If I Knew . . .
Digital art — Photoshop
 2011 Rafi

WORDS

If I Knew

If I knew it would be the last time I'd
see you walk out the door,
I'd give you a big hug and kiss and
then call you back for more.

I didn't think it would be the last time
I'd be there to share your day.
I was sure we'd have many more,
so I could let this one slip away.

For surely there's tomorrow
to make up for an oversight,
and don't we always get a second chance
to make everything just right?

But just in case I might be wrong,
and today is all I get,
I'd like to say how much I love you, and
I hope you don't forget.

If you're waiting for tomorrow
to say it, why not do it today?
For if tomorrow never comes,
you'll surely regret the day

You didn't take the extra time
for a smile, a hug, or kiss;
or that you were too busy to grant
what turned out to be one last wish.

Take time to say, "I'm sorry,"
"Please forgive me," "Thank you," or "It's OK."
And if tomorrow never comes,
you'll have no regrets about today.

Originally titled "Tomorrow Never Comes," this poem was written by Norma Cornett Marek in 1989 as a tribute to a child she lost. She released all copyright restrictions. Michael Grossman subsequently copyrighted the poem. You can see this poem in a PowerPoint presentation and hear a beautiful musical accompaniment. Google "Tomorrow Never Comes."

Peter Pan. . . I Belive

Digital art

2011 Rafi

WORDS

Every one of us is guided by our beliefs. Our beliefs lead us, determine what we do, and form our character. You can change; you can change your beliefs. Try these.

I Believe

We don't have to change friends if we understand that friends change. No matter how good a friend is, they're going to hurt you every once in a while and you must forgive them for that.

You can do something in an instant that will give you heartache for life. You should always leave loved ones with loving words. It may be the last time you see them.

You can keep going long after you can't.

We are responsible for what we do, no matter how we feel.

Either you control your attitude or it controls you.

Heroes are the people who do what has to be done when it needs to be done, regardless of the consequences.

Money is a lousy way of keeping score.

Sometimes the people you expect to kick you when you're down will be the ones to help you get back up.

Sometimes when I'm angry I have the right to be angry, but that doesn't give me the right to be cruel.

Just because someone doesn't love you the way you want them to doesn't mean they don't love you with all they have.

It isn't always enough to be forgiven by others. Sometimes you have to learn to forgive yourself

No matter how bad your heart is broken, the world doesn't stop for your grief. Just because two people argue doesn't mean they don't love each other and just because they don't argue, it doesn't mean they do.

You shouldn't be eager to find out a secret. It could change your life forever.

Two people can look at the exact same thing and see something totally different.

Your life can be changed in a matter of hours by people who don't even know you.

Even when you think you have no more to give, when a friend cries out to you, you will find the strength to help.

The people you care about most in life are taken from you too soon.

These words are probably the most important advice you've ever received.

Old Fly Fisherman

Study for a painting 18x24 charcoal paper

© 2011 Rafi

WORDS

Blessed In Aging
~Esther Mary Walker

Blessed are they who understand my
faltering step and shaking hand.
Blessed, who know my ears today
must strain to hear the things they say.
Blessed are those who seem to know
my eyes are dim and my mind is slow.
Blessed are those who looked away
when I spilled tea that weary day.
Blessed are they who, with cheery smile,
stopped to chat for a little while.
Blessed are they who know the way
to bring back memories of yesterday.
Blessed are those who never say,
"You've told that story twice today."
Blessed are they who make it known
that I am loved, respected and not alone.
And blessed are they who will ease the days
of my journey home, in loving ways.

This poem was read by Mary Maxwell in the video, "A Reminder That Laughter is the Best Medicine."

A Personal Life-enhancing Affirmation

Written by Father Tom Monahan

I *(enter your name)*, am of great value because I am life expressing itself. I like myself. I appreciate myself, and I am the beloved son of God in whom He is well pleased. I do good; I intend good; I am good.

I have unlimited potential and I enjoy activating my potential. I am filled with curiosity, and I have the energy, the focus and the persistence to achieve the answers I am searching for. I truly value and care for all human beings. I remember peoples' names and faces because I like them. I greet people with a smile and silently think, "May God bless you." I put the very best interpretation possible on other peoples' actions; and I never criticize someone behind their back. I point out their good qualities.

When I talk to a person, I remember that he or she is a special child of God. I show them great respect by listening carefully to what they say and don't say. Should I find myself becoming upset or angry at their comments, I take a deep breath and begin asking open-ended questions that allow them to expand more fully on their views. My goal is to build a relationship based upon trust, openness, acceptance, sincerity and truth.

I meet all life's challenges very creatively and with easy success. I do only those activities that produce good health in mind and body. I live in a worshipful relationship with the Lord Jesus Christ in the here and now with easy self-confidence, calm courage, great hope, magnificent joy and a heart filled with gratitude for God's grace.

This piece was shared with me by my friend, Cal Johnson, Houston, Texas. Cal said, "These affirmations were developed during a 12-hour course at the University of St. Thomas in the spring of 1981 which was taught by Father Tom Monahan. Father Tom had a PhD in clinical psychology and had taught and practiced for over 50 years. He passed away some years ago.

I will never forget him and what he taught me about life and humanity."

W O R D S

Don't Shortcut Experience

Don't shortcut experience.

Having one repair, one construction,

one surgery, is better than no experience.

However, having 100 repetitions of a

dangerous or risky task is infinitely better.

Go for experience.

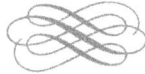

Your Personal "Bucket List"

Your bucket list represents a list of things you want to do while you're still alive. Make your own list. The list below is a starter; place a mark by all the things you want in your personal list and add other things. The bucket list applies to your entire life!

START doing them!

Get married/divorced
Bail out of a plane
Go hiking
Be kissed under mistletoe
Go to (you fill in the place)
Go skinny dipping outdoors
Go fishing
Go boating
Go flying in a hot air balloon
Get lost with someone I love
Go camping in a trailer/RV
Pilot a plane
Go bungee-jumping
Blow bubbles in a public place
Have my body pierced
Camp out under the stars
Catch snowflakes on my tongue
Color with crayons
Dance in the rain
Ride an elephant
Be on a TV show.
Eat just cookies for dinner

Watch a favorite movie...again
How many times will you watch it?
Sample and choose a favorite dessert
Fly in a glider
Fly in a plane doing acrobatics
Fly in a biplane
Furthest place I want to drive in a car
Go on a blind date (if single!)
Go to a drive-in movie
Go skiing
Have an indoor pet
Make prank phone calls
Pay for an expensive meal with coins
Sing with a Western band
Sing Karaoke at a sleazy bar
Serve on a murder trial jury
Shoot a gun
Swim in the ocean with Dolphins
Take a vacation alone
Watch a sunrise with someone you love
Experiment and choose a favorite drink

One of The Great Secrets of Our Times

Here's the great success secret: Put Pareto's law to work for you.

If you do, you will be able to spend your energies on the really important things in every aspect of your life. Pareto's Law will enable you to zero in on activities that produce the most beneficial results. The "80/20 Rule," as Pareto's Law is referred to today, works. It should be used by every person in their daily life, and by every organization. The 80/20 Rule can be applied to almost anything. Using the 80/20 Rule, major achievements increase with much less effort. The 80/20 Rule can raise personal effectiveness and happiness. It can impact on the profitability of corporations and the effectiveness of an organization. It holds the key to raising the quality and quantity of services, and, at the same time, cutting costs. Following Pareto's Law enables its users to achieve outstanding accomplishments.

What Is Pareto's Law or the 80/20 Rule?

The 80/20 Rule tells us that in any situation, some results are more important than others and deserve our attention. In most cases, 80% of results come from 20% of happenings. Stated another way: 20% of all efforts result in 80% of accomplishments. Also implied is that, in many cases, achieving 100% is not efficient. Near-perfection efficiency is, relatively speaking, much more expensive. It may be prohibitively so. Everyday language is a good illustration of the 80/20 Rule. Sir Isaac Pitman, who invented shorthand, discovered that just 700 common words make up 80% of words used in conversation. Although some dictionaries list over half a million words, Pitman found that the 700 words are used in 80% of common speech. He also concluded that less than one percent of the 700 words are used 80% of the time. That's seven words! Similarly, over 99% of talk uses fewer than 20% of the 700-word vocabulary. That's 140 words!

The internal combustion engine also illustrates the principle. 80% of the energy an engine creates is wasted in combustion; only 20% gets to the wheels. This 20% of the energy input generates 100% of the output!

Examples of the 80/20 Rule *(from many sources):*

Nationally:

> 80% of the wealth is owned by 20% of the people.
>
> 80% of outputs result from 20% of inputs.
>
> 80% of consequences flow from 20% of causes.
>
> 80% of results come from 20% of effort.
>
> 80% of earthquakes are small; 20% are big
>
> 80% of cities are small

The top 5% to 15% of U.S. long-distance callers make 55% to 60% of all long-distance calls.

In business:

> 20% of products account for 80% of dollar sales.
>
> 20% of products account for 80% of an organization's profits.
>
> 20% of stock takes up 80% of warehouse space.
>
> 20% of customers account for 80% of dollar sales.
>
> 20% of customers account for 80% of an organization's profits.
>
> 20% of advertising yields 80% of a campaign's results.
>
> 20% of staff will provide 80% of production.
>
> 20% of staff will cause 80% of problems.
>
> 80% of profit is achieved from 20% of the customers (not necessarily the same 20% as the ones who are responsible for 80% of sales).
>
> 80% of inventory represents 20% of all products.
>
> 10% of a bank's retail customers can represent 90% of its retail profits.
>
> 80% of customer complaints are about the same 20% of projects, products or services.
>
> 80% of stock comes from 20% of suppliers.
>
> 80% of sales are made by 20% of sales staff.
>
> 80% of box office revenues are from a third of movies produced.

In the car rental industry, the top 0.5% of customers rent 25% of cars.

A small amount of the code of a computer program is sufficient to process almost all situations. The bulk of the code (more than 95%) handles exceptions that occur in less than 5% of the cases.

W O R D S

In society:

20% of criminals account for 80% of the value of all crime.

20% of motorists cause 80% of accidents.

20% of those who marry comprise 80% of the divorce statistics (those who consistently remarry and divorce distort the statistics and give a lopsidedly pessimistic impression of marital fidelity).

In the home:

20% of carpets are likely to get 80% of the wear.

20% of clothes will be worn 80% of the time.

If a home has an intruder alarm, 80% of the false alarms will be set off by 20% of the possible causes.

Personally:

Helping the good 80% improve is a better use of time than helping the great 20% become terrific.

If you have ten things to do, two of those are usually worth as much as the other eight put together.

Of the things you do, you probably always know what activities will produce the greatest results. Concentrate on them and ignore the others.

80% of job achievements come from 20% of the time spent! That means four-fifths of a work day's effort, a dominant part of it, is largely irrelevant.

The 80/20 Lesson

There is a lack of balance between causes and results, inputs and outputs, and effort and reward. The 80/20 Rule proves, without doubt, that the universe is predictably unbalanced.

The lesson is that only a few things really matter. Only a few things cause significant changes. A minority of causes, inputs or efforts usually lead to a majority of the results, outputs or rewards.

Make the powerful forces of this principle work. The value of the Pareto Principle is the understanding of the importance of focusing on the 20% that matters; that 20% of something produces 80% of results. There are opportunities everywhere to apply the principle.

Separate major causes from the minor ones. Tackle the major causes or opportunities first; don't spend time on the minor issues. The 80/20 Rule has been tested over the years and has proved a sound business practice.

Make choices that maximize productivity. Give as few resources as possible to those tasks which produce the least. Understand the value of choices, use the statistics and success will result.

The Discovery of Pareto's Law

Vilfredo Pareto (1848-1923), a noted economist and sociologist best known for his Law of Income Distribution, is the originator of the concept, aptly named "Pareto's Law." Pareto is credited with being one of the first to analyze economic problems. In 1897 his research indicated that 80% of the land in Italy was owned by 20% of the population. He also noted that 20% of the population had 80% of the capital. This was the first instance of a socio-economic law that appeared to have universal application. The concept has helped to shape the modern world.

Pareto's second finding was that this pattern of imbalance was repeated consistently.

Pareto's Law assumes that 20% of something is far more important than the other 80% of something, because it provides 80% of the returns. He also observed that the cost required to move from 80% to 100% of the objective is four times greater than the cost required to move from 0% to 80%.

Paretos' work has been substantiated by many others, principally by George Kingsley Zipf and Dr. Joseph M. Juran.

Zipf, a Harvard professor of philology, discovered in 1949 the "Power Law," which was actually a rediscovery and elaboration of Pareto's Law.

He observed that small occurrences are extremely common, whereas large occurrences are extremely rare. He stated that approximately 20-30% of any resource accounted for 70-80% of the activity related to that resource. Many man-made and naturally occurring phenomena also demonstrate this Power Law distribution principle. For example, there are few large earthquakes but many small ones. There are a few mega-cities, but many small towns. Professor Zipf used population statistics, books, philology and industrial behavior to show the consistent recurrence of this unbalanced pattern.

Zipf showed there are a few words, such as yes, no, how, the, in, on, above, outside, over, under, he, she, we, etc., that occur very frequently in language, but there are many others which occur rarely. As a linguist, Zipf observed that with hundreds of thousands of words in the English language, it typically takes a lifetime to achieve a masterful vocabulary. However, to achieve fluency, it is only necessary to learn the most common 2,500 words and that a small percentage of the common words is responsible for over 95% of communication.

In the late 1940s, quality management pioneer, Dr. Joseph Juran, recognized a universal principle he called the "vital few and the useful many." It was recognition of Pareto's Law or the 80/20 Rule." He also gave voice to something project managers know: that 20% of a project (the first 10% and the last 10%) consume 80% of time and resources.

References

The following books and/or articles provided valuable insight in the preparation of this article:

Narula, Avinash, *What is 80/20 Rule, Pareto's Law, Pareto Principle*

Newman, MEJ. *Power laws, Pareto Distributions, and Zipf's law.*

Rooney, Paula (October 3, 2002), *Microsoft's CEO: 80-20 Rule Applies To Bugs, Not Just Features*, ChannelWeb.

Taleb, Nassim (2007), *The Black Swan*, pp. 228–252, 274–285.

Klass, O. S.; Biham, O.; Levy, M.; Malcai, O.; Soloman, S. (2006), *The Forbes 400 and the Pareto wealth distribution*, Economics Letters 90 (2): 290–295

Koch, R. (2001), *The 80/20 Principle: The Secret of Achieving More with Less*, London: Nicholas Brealey Publishing.

Koch, R. (2004), *Living the 80/20 Way: Work Less, Worry Less, Succeed More, Enjoy More*, London: Nicholas Brealey Publishing.

Reed, W. J. (2001), *The Pareto, Zipf and Other Power Laws*, Economics Letters 74 (1): 15–19.

Searle, Edith, *New Era Shorthand: Basic Business Dictation*, Longman Publishing.

Cornucopia

Painting 20x16 Acrylic on canvas

© 2011 Rafi

Clever Ideas Worth Knowing

Bananas. Take your bananas apart when you get home from the store. If you leave them connected at the stem, they ripen faster.

Store your opened chunks of cheese in aluminum foil. The cheese will stay fresh much longer and not mold! (Same thing for celery, plus it keeps it crisp!)

Peppers with 3 bumps on the bottom are sweeter and better for eating. Peppers with 4 bumps on the bottom are firmer and better for cooking.

Add a teaspoon of water when frying ground beef. It will help pull the grease away from the meat while cooking.

To really make scrambled eggs or omelets rich, add a couple of spoonfuls of sour cream, cream cheese, or heavy cream and then beat them together.

For a cool brownie treat, make brownies as directed. Then melt Andes mints in a double broiler and pour over warm brownies. Let set for a wonderful minty frosting.

Add garlic immediately to a recipe if you want a light taste of garlic. Add garlic at the end of the recipe if you want a stronger taste.

Leftover Snickers bars make a delicious dessert. Simply chop them up with the food chopper. Peel, core, and slice a few apples. Place them in a baking dish and sprinkle the chopped candy bars over the apples. Bake at 350 for 15 minutes. Serve alone or with vanilla ice cream.

Reheat leftover pizza in a nonstick skillet on top of the stove. Set heat to med-low and heat till warm. This keeps the crust crispy. No soggy micro pizza!

Easy deviled eggs. Put cooked egg yolks in a zip lock bag. Seal, mash till they are all broken up. Add remainder of ingredients, reseal, keep mashing it up, mixing thoroughly. Cut the tip off the baggy, squeeze mixture into eggs. Throw the bag away when done.

Broken glass. Use a wet cotton ball or Q-tip to pick up the small shards of glass you can't see easily.

Expanding frosting. When you buy a container of cake frosting from the store, whip it with your mixer for a few minutes. You can double it in size. You get to frost more cake/cupcakes with the same amount. You also eat less sugar and calories per serving.

Reheating refrigerated bread. To warm biscuits, pancakes, or muffins that were refrigerated, place them in a microwave with a cup of water. The increased moisture will keep the food moist and help it reheat faster.

Newspaper weeds away. After putting in your plants, work the nutrients in your soil. Then, wet the newspapers, put layers around the plants, overlapping as you go. Cover with mulch and forget about weeds. Weeds will get through some gardening plastic but they will not get through wet newspapers.

No more mosquitoes. Place a dryer sheet in your pocket. It will keep the mosquitoes away.

Squirrel away. To keep squirrels from eating your plants, sprinkle your plants with cayenne pepper. The cayenne pepper doesn't hurt the plant and the squirrels won't come near it.

Flexible vacuum. To get something out of a heat register or under the fridge, add an empty paper towel roll or empty gift wrap roll to your vacuum. It can be bent or flattened to get in narrow openings.

Reducing static cling. Pin a small safety pin to the seam of your slip and you will not have a clingy skirt or dress. Same thing works with slacks that cling when wearing panty hose. Place a pin in the seam of the slacks and ... Da Da! Static is gone.

Measuring cups. Before you pour sticky substances into a measuring cup, fill the cup with hot water. Dump out the hot water, but don't dry the cup. Next, add your ingredient, such as peanut butter, and watch how easily it comes right out.

Reopening envelopes. If you seal an envelope and then realize you forgot to include something inside, just place your sealed envelope in the freezer for an hour or two. Viola! It unseals easily.

Foggy windshield? Hate foggy windshields? Buy a chalkboard eraser and keep it in the glove box of your car. When the windows fog, rub with the eraser. Works better than a cloth.

Hair conditioner shaving lotion. Ladies, use hair conditioner to shave your legs. It's cheaper than shaving cream and leaves your legs really smooth. It's also a great way to use up the conditioner you bought but didn't like when you tried it in your hair.

Goodbye fruit flies. To get rid of pesky fruit flies, take a small glass, fill it half full with Apple Cider Vinegar and 2 drops of dish washing liquid; mix well. The flies will be drawn to the cup and gone forever!

W O R D S

Get rid of ants. Put small piles of cornmeal where you see ants. They eat it, take it 'home,' can't digest it, so it kills them. It may take a week or so, especially if it rains, but it works and you don't have the worry about pets or small children being harmed!

Clothes dryers. If the heating unit on your dryer goes out, the first thing to do is pull out the lint filter. Even if the filter looks clean, take the filter over to the sink and run hot water over it to see if the hot water sits on top of the mesh filter. Dryer sheets can cause a film to build up over the mesh.

It's caused by what's in the dryer sheets to make your clothes soft and static free and create that nice fragrance. The stuff builds up on your clothes and on your lint screen. Wash the filter with hot soapy water and a brush at least every six months.

Where did all this stuff come from? I have no idea.

This short article is based on Mitch Albon's book, "Tuesdays with Morrie," published by Broadway Books in 1997. Many quotes from the book are included within the article. The lessons are so powerful; I want to share with you some that continue to influence my life. I get courage as I remember Morrie Schwartz.

Every Moment Before You Die

A dying person will probably want to squeeze out every moment possible with loved ones. Those of us not concerned with dying seem to spend our time doing things that are completely meaningless.

Envy someone who can be so focused they can ignore everything else except their death. With each passing day, available time diminishes. Not led by a dying timetable, we spend our time distracted by unimportant things. Why? Why do we give up days and weeks of our lives addicted to someone else's drama?

The culture that sets the rules for our lives mentally penalizes us when we try to feel good about ourselves. But we can ignore the culture. We **can** feel good about ourselves. Refuse to buy into a culture that doesn't make life better. Do the things that emphasize goodness: things like kindness, loving, forgiving, new ideas, friendships, letter writing, reading books, participating in discussion groups, joyful dancing, long walks, leisurely meals, good wine, enjoying nature, rainy afternoons, lying in bed with someone you love, moonlight, sunsets, and on and on. Fill your life. Fill it like an overflowing soup bowl.

Doesn't it seem some people have a meaningless life? They like to think they're doing something important, but the truth is they're chasing the wrong things. The way you get meaning into your life is by devoting yourself to loving others, devoting yourself to the community around you, and devoting yourself to creating something that gives you purpose and meaning.

Giving out love and letting love come in may well be the most important things in life.

Lao-Tzu said, "We are most alive when we're in love. Being deeply loved by someone gives you strength. Loving someone deeply gives you courage."

So many think they don't deserve love. They're afraid that if they let love in, they'll become too soft. But, as Stephen Levine said, "love is the only rational act."

Morrie said, "Everyone knows they're going to die, but nobody believes it. If we did, we would do things differently." How can you ever be prepared to die?

Here's a better approach: Believe you're going to die. **You don't know**

when you're going to die. But you can be prepared for it at any time. The preparing enables a person to be more involved in life while living. Do what the Buddhists do. Every day a little bird sits on a Buddhist's shoulder asking, "Is today the day? Is today the day I am going to die? Am I ready? Am I doing all I need to do? Am I being the person I want to be?"

Once you learn how to die, you learn how to live. Most of us walk around as if we're sleepwalking. That lack-of-attention keeps us from experiencing the world fully; we do the things we do automatically because we think we have to.

Most of us have a foundation. It's Safe Ground. It's a place where we're loved without reservation. It's secure ground. It's **family.**

Who else besides your family gives you love and support and caring and concern? Your family truly loves you.

If we don't love one another, we perish. (W. H. Auden said it, "Love each other or perish.")

Isn't it great to know there's someone out there watching out for you? That's a true demonstration of love. It's spiritual maturity. It's family.

Wine, Fruit and Cheese. .

Digital art

© 2011 Rafi

This dessert is adapted from the Brennan family's Palace Cafe, in New Orleans. We have had guests describe this dish as "the best dessert I've ever had!

White Chocolate Bread Pudding
with White Chocolate Sauce (serves 6)

THE PUDDING

8 ounces French bread, cut into 1-inch pieces without crust

18 ounces good-quality white chocolate (such as Lindt or Baker's), coarsely chopped (morsels are OK)

3 1/2 cups whipping cream

1 cup milk (do not use low-fat or nonfat)

7 large egg yolks

2 large eggs

1/2 cup sugar

Preheat oven to 275° F. Arrange bread cubes on baking sheet. Bake until light golden and dry, about 10-15 minutes. Transfer baking sheet to rack; cool completely. Increase oven temperature to 350F°.

Combine 3 cups whipping cream, 1 cup milk and 1/2 cup sugar in a heavy large saucepan. Bring to simmer over medium heat, stirring until the sugar dissolves. Remove from heat. Add 10 ounces of the white chocolate (about 1 3/4 cups) and stir until melted and smooth.

Whisk yolks and eggs in large bowl to blend. Gradually whisk in the warm chocolate mixture.

Place bread cubes in a 2-quart glass baking dish. Add half of chocolate mixture. Press bread cubes into chocolate mixture. Let stand until bread is completely soaked through, about 15 minutes. Gently mix in remaining chocolate mixture. Cover dish with foil. Bake pudding 45 minutes. Uncover and bake until top is golden brown, about 15 minutes. Transfer pudding to rack and cool slightly. Cover over with foil and refrigerate. Re-warm covered pudding in 350F° oven for 30 minutes before serving.

WHITE CHOCOLATE SAUCE

Bring remaining 1/2 cup cream to simmer in heavy medium saucepan. Remove saucepan from heat. Add remaining 8 ounces white chocolate and stir until melted and smooth.

Serve pudding warm with warm white chocolate sauce. Both the pudding and the sauce can be prepared ahead, refrigerated and reheated in the microwave.

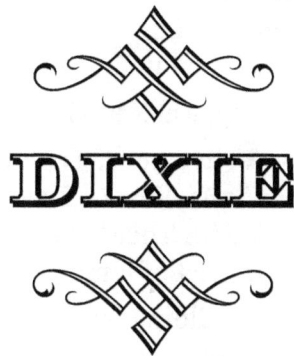

DIXIE

CAN YOU HAVE A
DIXIELAND FUNERAL?

Of course you can. After all, it's your funeral. You're the Star and the Director.

The traditional Dixieland Funeral, styled after those in New Orleans, is a joyful celebration of life. New Orleans music began when the military march beat was liberated from the soldiers and given to lovers, party-goers, and mourners. The music is a reflection of the influence of the many cultures that have made New Orleans one of the most exciting cities in America and is uniquely a product of the United States. Musical instruments typically associated with a marching Dixieland band are the trumpet, coronet, clarinet, soprano sax, alto sax, trombone, tuba, banjo, and snare drum. When playing does not involve marching, a piano and a bass drum are included in the ensemble.

Here are the characteristics of a typical New Orleans funeral celebration:

• Following the funeral service, live music is played by a Dixieland Jazz band (also referred to as *Classic Jazz* or *Traditional Jazz).* Favorite tunes are "Just A Closer Walk with Thee" and "When the Saints Go Marching In." See the following list of famous Dixieland tunes.

• The music starts outside the building where the funeral service was held (it could be a home, a church, a funeral home, or a rented hall).

• The parade begins as mourners, other relatives of the family, friends, and neighbors gather in a loose parade formation for the march to the graveyard. This is the "Main Line."

• The Dixieland Jazz Band leads the procession. (*If you're contemplating doing this in your town, as a practical matter, since many cemeteries are a long way from the place where the celebration of a life lived service will be held, a shorter route makes sense. Consider marching from the church through the parking lot and around the church a time or two. It doesn't matter how long the parade lasts, it's the parade protocol that makes it a funeral march.)*

• The band plays somber, sad hymns at the beginning of the march.
• There is a point where the band leader makes a distinct break with playing the sad refrains, typically after either the deceased is buried, or the hearse leaves the procession or the "paid" clock is about to end. The change in tempo means the mourners have said their final good-byes and are beginning to change the tenor of the celebration. This stage is called "cuttin' the body loose." The procession has finished

WORDS

saying their good-byes and is ready to welcome their friend to a better and happier life in heaven.

• The music beat changes. The band begins playing hymns in a typical "swinging" Dixieland style. Popular New Orleans favorites are played.

• The upbeat music continues; a little louder and faster. It's a joyful soul-movin' sound. The funeral party and onlookers join the celebration.

• Onlookers, called the "Second Line," follow the Main Line and the band for the music and the opportunity to dance with the crowd. Twirling a parasol or waving a handkerchief in the air is part of the "second lining."

If the church's policies' permit, a natural extension of the band's contribution to the funeral celebration is having them provide the music during the service.

DIXIELAND TUNES

Ace in the Hole

After I Say I'm Sorry

After You've Gone

Ain't Misbehavin'

Alabama Jubilee

Alexander's Ragtime Band

All of Me

As I Lay My Burden Down

At A Georgia Camp Meeting

At the Jazz Band Ball

Avalon

Baby Face

Basin Street Blues

Big Butter and Egg Man

Black Bottom Stomp

Blue Skies

Blues My Naughty Sweetie

Buddy's Habits

Bye Bye Blackbird

Bye Bye Blues

Cabaret

Canal Street Blues

Caravan

Charleston

Chicago

China Boy

Copenhagen

Darktown Strutter's Ball

Dead Man Blues

Feel So Good

Dinah

Dippermouth Blues

Do Me Like You Do

Do You Know What It Means

Down by the Riverside

Dr. Jazz

Everybody Loves My Baby

Farewell Blues

Fidgety Feet

Five-Foot-Two

Georgia

Goody Goody

Hello, Dolly!

High Society

Honeysuckle Rose

How Come You Do

I Can't Give You Anything But Love

I Found A New Baby

Ice Cream

In the Sweet Bye and Bye

Indiana

Irish Black Bottom

Is It True What They Say About Dixie?

It Don't Mean A Thing

I've Got Rhythm

Just a Closer Walk With Thee

Lady Be Good

Mack, the Knife!

Mama's Gone, Goodbye

Margie

Midnight in Moscow

Milenberg Joys

Mississippi Mud

Muskrat Ramble

My Gal Sal
Oh, Baby!
Oh, Didn't He Ramble
On the Sunny Side
Of The Street
Panama
Potato Head Blues
Putting On the Ritz
Riverboat Shuffle
Rose of Washington
Square
Rosetta
Royal Garden Blues
Sailin' Down the
Chesapeake Bay
Saint James
Infirmary Blues
San Antonio Rose
Sensation Rag
Shanty Town
Sheik of Araby

Shim-Me-Sha-Wabble
Street Parade
St. Louis Blues
Stars Fell On Alabama
Struttin' With Some
Barbecue
Swanee
Sweet Georgia Brown
Swing That Music
That Da-Da Strain
The Crave
That's A Plenty
There'll Be Some
Changes Made

Thou Swell
Tiger Rag
Tin Roof Blues
Undecided
Up A Lazy River
Waitin' For The
Robert E. Lee
Walk Through
The Streets Of
The City
Washington and
Lee Swing
Way Down Yonder
In New Orleans
When My Sugar
Walks Down
The Street
When the Saints
Go Marching In
When You're
Smiling
Yellow Rose
Of Texas

THE GIANTS OF JAZZ
(as listed by birthdate in Wikipedia)

Jazz, as an "American" innovation, continues to impact music of the 2000's. However, the style was at its pinnacle in the late 1800's and early 1900's. The history of the movement will always include these "giants"

Instrumentalists

Scott Joplin (1868–1917)
Charles "Buddy" Bolden (1877–1931)
Duke Ellington (1899–1974)
Louis Armstrong (1901–71)
Earl Hines (1903–83)
Fats Waller (1904–43)
Count Basie (1904–84)
Benny Goodman (1909–86)
Sun Ra (1914–93)
Thelonious Monk (1917–82)
Dizzy Gillespie (1917–93)
Charlie Parker (1920–55)
Dave Brubeck (born 1920)
Charles Mingus (1922–79)
Oscar Peterson (1925–2007)
Miles Davis (1926–91)
John Coltrane (1926–67)
Chet Baker (1929–88)
Ornette Coleman (born 1930)

Vocalists

Louis Armstrong (1901–71)
Billie Holiday (1915–59)
Ella Fitzgerald (1917–96)
Dinah Washington (1924-63)
Sarah Vaughan (1924–90)
Nina Simone (1933-2003)

WORDS

CANCER

BY THE NUMBERS—THE 10 DEADLIEST CANCERS
Adapted from an article by Amanda Chan

The dread and fear that can come with a cancer diagnosis have their roots in its killer nature. According to the Centers for Disease Control and Prevention, cancer is the second cause of death in Americans, preceded by heart disease. Even when diagnosed early and attacked with the latest treatments, it still has the power to kill.

While there are many successful treatments today that didn't exist just a couple decades ago, a cure for cancer remains elusive. There are more than 100 types of cancer, all characterized by abnormal cell growth. There are many different causes, ranging from radiation to chemicals to viruses.

How cancer cells grow is a mystery that is yet to be completely solved. Cell growth is an ingenious problem, unpredictable and in some cases mysterious. Even after seemingly effective treatments, crafty cancer cells are able to hide out in some patients and resurface.

About $200 billion has been spent on cancer research since the early 1970s, and the five-year survival rate for all people diagnosed with cancer in the U.S. has risen from about 50 percent in the 1970s to 65 percent today.

Here's a fast look at the 10 cancers that killed the most people in the United States between 2003 and 2007. (The numbers shown are the totals from 2003 to the end of 2007.)

1. Lung and bronchial cancer: 792,495 lives
Lung and bronchial cancer is the top killer cancer in the United States. Smoking and use of tobacco products are the major causes of it, and it strikes most often between the ages of 55 and 65. There are two major types: non-small cell lung cancer, which is the most common, and small cell lung cancer, which spreads more quickly.

2. Colon and rectal cancer: 268,783 lives
Colon cancer grows in the tissues of the colon, whereas rectal cancer grows in the last few inches of the large intestine near the anus. Most cases begin as clumps of small, benign cells called polyps that over time become cancerous. Screening is recommended to find the polyps before they become cancerous.

3. Breast cancer: 206,983 lives
Breast cancer is the second most common cancer in women in the United States, after skin cancer. It can also occur in men – there were nearly 2,000 male cases between 2003 and 2008. The cancer usually forms in the ducts that carry milk to the nipple or the glands that produce the milk in women.

4. Pancreatic cancer: 162,878 lives
Pancreatic cancer begins in the tissues of the pancreas, which aids digestion and metabolism regulation. Detection and early intervention are difficult because it often progressives stealthily and rapidly.

5. Prostate cancer: 144,926 lives

This cancer is the second-leading cause of cancer deaths in men, after lung and bronchial cancer. Prostate cancer usually starts to grow slowly in the prostate gland, which produces the seminal fluid to transport sperm. Some types remain confined to the gland, and are easier to treat, but others are more aggressive and spread quickly.

6. Leukemia: 108,740 lives

There are many types of leukemia, but all affect the blood-forming tissues of the body, such as the bone marrow and the lymphatic system, and result in an overproduction of abnormal white blood cells. Leukemia types are classified by how fast they progress and which cells they affect. A type called *acute myelogenous leukemia* killed the most people–41,714– between 2003 and 2007.

7. Non-Hodgkin lymphoma: 104,407 lives

This cancer affects the lymphocytes, a type of white blood cell, and is characterized by larger lymph nodes, fever and weight loss. There are several types of non-Hodgkin lymphoma, and they are categorized by whether the cancer is fast or slow-growing and which types of lymphocytes are affected. Non-Hodgkin lymphoma is deadlier than Hodgkin lymphoma.

8. Liver and intrahepatic bile duct cancer: 79,773 lives

Liver cancer is one of the most common forms of cancer around the world, but is uncommon in the United States. However, its rates in America are rising. Most liver cancer that occurs in the U.S. begins elsewhere and then spreads to the liver. A closely related cancer is bile duct cancer, which occurs in the duct that carries bile from the liver to the small intestine.

9. Ovarian cancer: 73,638 lives

 Ovarian cancer was the No. 4 cause of cancer death in women between 2003 and 2007. The median age of women diagnosed with it is 63. The cancer is easier to treat but harder to detect in its early stages, but recent research has brought light to early symptoms that may aid in diagnosis. Those symptoms include abdominal discomfort, urgency to urinate and pelvic pain.

10. Esophageal cancer: 66,659 lives

This cancer starts in the cells that line the esophagus (the tube that carries food from the throat to the stomach) and usually occurs in the lower part of the esophagus. More men than women died from esophageal cancer between 2003 and 2007.

The following report has been collected from a variety of sources. The information is believed to be accurate, but cannot be guaranteed. Everything seems to indicate progress in understanding cancer and cancer treatment. In summary: it's good reading, but check with your doctor to confirm any conclusions you draw from the data.

A 2010 CANCER UPDATE

Cancer is a genetic disease resulting from a variety of mutations and alterations either inherited from our parents or, more commonly, acquired over time due to environmental exposures and behaviors, such as smoking and poor diet. These alterations turn off important cell growth regulators, allowing cells to continually divide unchecked. This type of cell is called a malignant or cancer cell. Among the trillions of cells in the human body, inevitably everyone has some abnormal or atypical cells that possess some of the characteristics of cancer cells. Most resolve themselves and never result in cancer.

There is no single or standard test for cancer. There are ways to screen for certain cancers with tests such as colonoscopy for colon cancer, mammography for breast cancer, PSA for prostate cancer, and the Pap smear for cervical cancer. These tests can detect cancers in a very early and curable stage. For many cancers, there currently are no screening tests, and they are diagnosed when they begin to cause symptoms.

Cancer researchers are working on new tests that detect abnormal DNA shed by cancer cells into blood and body fluids. These tests have the ability to find cancers before they cause any symptoms. Approaches like this could lead to a broad-based screening test for cancer.

Tests like these also are being used to detect cancer recurrences and malignant cells left behind following surgery. The tests can find cancers that are not detectable under the microscope or in x-rays.

Other researchers are studying cancer stem cells. They are stealth cells that make up just a tiny fraction of a tumor. While small in number, investigators believe they may be the cells that drive certain cancers and lead to cancer recurrence. Therapies that target these cells are now being tested in clinical trials.

A team of breast cancer researchers has developed a method that could make it possible to detect breast cancer from the DNA contained in a single drop of blood.

Evasive cancer cells are a challenge and the focus of ongoing research. There is no support for the idea that all of us, even those treated successfully for cancer, have cancers-in-waiting, undetectable, but still there. People are treated and completely cured of cancer every day.

When it comes to cancer and the immune system, it is not a matter of strong or weak, but rather an issue of recognition. The immune system simply does not recognize cancer. In its complexity, the cancer cell has learned to disguise itself to the immune system as a normal, healthy cell. Cells infected with viruses or bacteria send out danger signals setting the immune system in action. But cancer cells do not. By deciphering the methods cancer cells use to make

WORDS

them invisible to the immune system, cancer vaccines have been developed that trigger immune reactions against prostate cancer, pancreatic cancer, leukemia, and multiple myeloma.

Dietary habits and lifestyle choices, such as smoking, contribute to the development of many human cancers. Experts recommend a balanced diet as a way of reducing cancer risk. In terms of supplements, while they may help mediate vitamin deficiencies, taking doses above what the body needs provides no added benefit.

Chemotherapy and radiation therapy kill cancer cells with remarkable selectivity. There are some temporary and reversible side effects common to cancer therapies, including hair loss and low blood counts. Limiting and managing these side effects is an integral part of treatment.

Surgery is the first line of treatment for many types of cancer. It does not cause cancer to spread. Cancers spread to other tissues and organs as a tumor progresses and cancer cells break away from the original tumor and travel through the bloodstream to other body sites.

According to the experts, a poor diet and obesity associated with a poor diet are risk factors for the development of cancer. However, there is no evidence that certain foods alter the environment of an existing cancer, at the cellular level, and cause it to either die or grow.

While there is such a thing as tumors that produce mucus, the mucus made by a tumor does not result from drinking milk. And, eating less meat, while a good choice for cancer prevention, does not free up enzymes to attack cancer cells.

Moderation is key. As part of a balanced diet, sugar, salt, milk, coffee, tea, meat, and chocolate are all safe choices. The real concern with many of these, particularly sugar, is that it adds calories to a diet and can lead to obesity, and obesity is a major risk factor for cancer. A balanced nutritious diet, healthy weight, physical activity, and avoiding alcoholic drinks may prevent as many as a third of all cancers. Try to eat at least five servings of fruits and vegetables per day and limit red and processed meats, like hot dogs.

The World Cancer Research Fund American Institute for Cancer Research published a report in November 2007, titled, "Food, Nutrition, Physical Activity, and the Prevention of Cancer: A Global Perspective." The report is considered be an authoritative source of information on diet, physical activity and cancer. Their recommendations for cancer prevention and for good health in general are:

1. Be as lean as possible without becoming underweight.
2. Be physically active for at least 30 minutes every day.
3. Avoid sugary drinks. Limit consumption of energy-dense foods (particularly processed foods high in added sugar or low in fiber, or high in fat).
4. Eat more of a variety of vegetables, fruits, whole grains and legumes such as beans.

5. Limit consumption of red meats (such as beef, pork and lamb) and avoid processed meats.

6. If consumed at all, limit alcoholic drinks to 2 for men and 1 for women a day.

7. Limit consumption of salty foods and foods processed with salt (sodium).

8. Don't use supplements to protect against cancer.

Experts recommend that people meet their nutritional needs through their food choices. While vitamin supplements can be helpful in people with nutritional deficiencies, evidence suggests that supplementation above what the body can use provides no added health benefit.

Cancer is a disease caused by genetic alterations. Many times these alterations occur through our own behaviors, such as cigarette smoking, a poor and unbalanced diet, virus exposures, and sunburns.

The influence of stress, faith, and other factors on cancer is largely unknown. While striving to be happy, loving, and stress free is a nice way to live and can contribute to an overall feeling of well-being, there is no evidence that a person prevents or causes cancer based on his or her state of mind.

Still, a cancer diagnosis can make patients and families feel stressed and anxious...not pleasant feelings. There are many services available to patients in addition to extensive patient and family services. For example, cancer counseling, pain and palliative care, chaplain services, a meditation chapel, an image recovery center, and an Art of Healing art and music program, all contribute to reducing stress and anxiety.

Regular exercise should be a part of any healthy lifestyle, but there is no evidence that breathing deeply or receiving oxygen therapy prevents cancer.

WORDS

For some, participation in a clinical trial is a cancer treatment option. MD Anderson, Houston, TX, one of the world's leading cancer research and treatment centers, uses clinical trials similar to the procedure described in this article.

SHOULD I TAKE PART IN A CLINICAL TRIAL AS PART OF MY CANCER TREATMENT?

Clinical trials are research studies in which patients may volunteer to take part. You should make a choice based on your health and your values. If you are offered a clinical trial, it is your right to decide whether to take part.

Clinical trials find better ways to prevent, diagnose and treat cancer. Doctors use treatment trials to learn more about how to fight cancer. Clinical trials are part of a long, careful process which may take many years.

First, doctors study a new treatment in the lab. Then they often study the treatment in animals. If the new treatment shows promise, doctors then test the treatment in people in strictly regulated phased clinical trials. Patients in clinical trials are protected by following well-planned protocols which:

- Explain the treatment plan
- List the medical tests patients will receive
- Give the number of patients taking part in the trial
- List eligibility criteria, which are guidelines to decide who may join the clinical trial
- Explain safety information

Patients are further protected through a careful informed consent process. Each protocol has strict rules, called eligibility criteria, which doctors must follow to decide who may join the clinical trial. The informed consent process and eligibility criteria protect patients from getting treatment that may harm them.

Eligibility criteria include information about:

- You and your overall health
- Age and gender
- Results of medical tests
- Medicines that you are taking
- Any other health problems
- Your cancer type and stage
- Other treatments you may have had
- How long it has been since you were last treated

If you have found a clinical trial you think you want to join, talk to your doctor to see if you are eligible. If eligible, you will be asked to sign a consent to participation form. The goal of informed consent is to make sure you understand the clinical trial's plan.

The doctor or research nurse will review the informed consent form in detail with you. This form explains the clinical trial's purpose, plan, risks and benefits.

This is a great time to ask questions. Consider bringing a family member or friend to help you ask questions and write down answers. You may also want to bring a tape recorder so that later you can listen to what the doctor said.

Take time to make your decision. If you like, take the informed consent form home with you to review before signing it.

Institutional Review Boards (IRBs) protect patients by reviewing protocols and monitoring trials. The IRBs are committees of doctors, nurses, chaplains, social workers, lawyers and patients. They make sure that trials follow federal laws and that patients are protected.

The U.S. Food and Drug Administration (FDA) audits the IRBs' files. Also, FDA officials may visit the research facility at any time and review anything they choose related to clinical trials.

Fun & Games

Here Are The Answers To 10 "Why?" Questions

1. Why are many coin banks shaped like pigs?
Long ago, dishes and cookware in Europe were made of a dense orange clay called 'pygg'. When people saved coins in jars made of this clay, the jars became known as 'pygg banks.' When an English potter misunderstood the word, he made a bank that resembled a pig. And it caught on.

2. Did you ever wonder why dimes, quarters and half dollars have notches, while pennies and nickels do not?
The US Mint began putting notches on the edges of coins containing gold and silver to discourage holders from shaving off small quantities of the precious metals. Dimes, quarters and half dollars are notched because they used to contain silver. Pennies and nickels aren't notched because the metals they contain are not valuable enough to shave.

3. Why do men's clothes have buttons on the right while women's clothes have buttons on the left?
When buttons were invented, they were very expensive and worn primarily by the rich. Because wealthy women were dressed by maids, dressmakers put the buttons on the maid's right! Since most people are right-handed, it is easier to push buttons on the right through holes on the left. And that's where women's buttons have remained since.

4. Why do X's at the end of a letter signify kisses?
In the Middle Ages, when many people were unable to read or write, documents were often signed using an X. Kissing the X represented an oath to fulfill obligations specified in the document. The X and the kiss eventually became synonymous.

5. Why is shifting responsibility to someone else called "passing the buck"?
In card games, it was once customary to pass an item, called a buck, from player to player to indicate whose turn it was to deal. If a player did not wish take the deal, he would 'pass the buck' to the next player.

6. Why do people clink their glasses before drinking a toast?
It used to be common for someone to try to kill an enemy by offering him a poisoned drink. To prove to a guest that a drink was safe, it became customary for a guest to pour a small amount of his drink into the glass of the host. Both men would drink it simultaneously. When a guest trusted his host, he would then just touch or clink the host's glass with his own.

W O R D S

7. Why are people in the public eye said to be "in the limelight"?
Invented in 1825, limelight was used in lighthouses and stage lighting by burning a cylinder of lime which produced a brilliant light. In the theatre, performers on stage 'in the limelight' were seen by the audience to be the center of attention.

8. Why do ships and aircraft in trouble use "mayday" as a call for help?
This comes from the French word m'aidez — meaning 'help me' — and is pronounced 'mayday.'

9. Why is someone who is feeling great "on cloud nine"?
Types of clouds are numbered according to the altitudes they attain, with nine being the highest cloud. If someone is said to be on cloud nine, that person is floating well above worldly cares.

10. Why are zero scores in tennis called "love"?
In France, where tennis first became popular, a big, round zero on the scoreboard looked like an egg and was called 'l'oeuf,' which is French for 'egg.' When tennis was introduced in the US , Americans pronounced it 'love.'

7 Tips For Remembering Names

Being able to remember names is a valuable asset in both the business and social arenas. It helps you build instant rapport with new contacts, and, as many companies place a premium on interpersonal and relationship-building skills, it makes a decidedly good impression on employers, too. So eliminate "whatshername" and 'whatshisface" from your vocabulary once and for all. The following techniques can help you remember the names of everyone you meet. The secret is repetition.

1. Be interested. Many of us don't even catch the other person's name when they're being introduced; we're too focused on ourselves. So the first step to remembering a name is to pay attention as you are introduced.

2. Verify. Unless the person has introduced himself to you, verify what he or she wishes to be called. At a conference or church, for example, the name tag may have been written illegibly or it may be a more formal or informal version of the name they like to go by. Or someone else may have introduced you who doesn't know the person well. Asking what they prefer (e.g. "Jeff introduced you as Debbie, is that what you prefer to be called?") will not only cement the name in your mind, but ensure you are using the name that pleases them.

3. Picture the name written across their forehead. Franklin Roosevelt continually amazed his staff by remembering the names of nearly everyone he met. His secret? He used to imagine seeing the name written across the person's forehead. This is a particularly powerful technique if you visualize the name written in your favorite color of Magic Marker.

4. Imagine writing the name. To take step three even further, neural linguistic programming experts suggest getting a feel for what it would be like to write the name by moving your finger in micro-muscle movements as you are seeing the name and saying it to yourself.

5. Relate the name. Try to associate a person's name with a familiar image or famous person. For example, if a woman's name is Jacqueline, picture her as Jacqueline Kennedy Onassis in a pink suit and pillbox hat. If a man's name is Arnold, imagine him as the "Terminator" or striking a body-builder pose.

6. Use it frequently. Try to use the name three or four times during your conversation. Use it when you first meet, when you ask a question and in your departure, (e.g., "Andrew, it was a pleasure talking to you. Maybe we'll get a chance to chat again sometime.")

WORDS

7. Record the name in a "new contacts" file. Top sales representatives keep a record of new contact names and information, including where and when they met. Review it now and then, especially when you will be attending a meeting where you may see these individuals again.

Summary Using these techniques will dramatically increase your ability to recall names, but it is inevitable that at one time or another you may slip up. If you do happen to run into someone whom you previously met and can't remember their name, you have two options:

- Look delighted to see them, lock eyes and extend a warm "Good to see you again," and then find out their name from a friend or guest list later.
- Or, with the same warmth, try the more direct, "I remember you well, but your name has slipped my mind."

I don't know who came up with these suggestions first. In trying to find out I discovered lots of people have suggestions to help remember names and faces. But these rules are great. And they work!

How Is Your Memory

Adapted from the Houston Chronicle, December 26th, 2010, Section G)

We live in a competitive culture. We keep score. Whatever it is we're doing, from taking tests to golf handicaps, we like to know how we measure up to others. And, as we grow older, the competitiveness doesn't end. We wonder whether others our age are doing as well as we are?
The Houston Chronicle adapted a series of six standardized tests from recognized sources for citizens 50+ to generally compare their abilities to others within their age group. This article is based on that newspaper article.

These tests are not rocket science. If you don't do too well on these short evaluations and you're worried, contact a trained clinician for cognitive and physiological tests.

Bur remember this: **if you are alert enough to take the tests and to be concerned about your score, that's good. You're still in the game!**

WORDS

Word Count

What it measures: Verbal fluency, mental organization, short-term memory
Test

For one minute, count how many words you can say beginning with the letter "F.

For another minute, say words starting with "A."

Then a third minute , words starting with "S."

Add them up. Don't use proper nouns, don't repeat words, no variations on the same word. (If you say "apple," you can't use "apples.")

Score:

On average, people aged:

50 to 59, listed 42 words

60 to 69, listed 38.5 words

70 to79, listed 35 words

80 to 90. listed 29 words

90 to 95, listed 28 words

Good to know

Unlike some other skills, vocabulary improves up to a fairly mature age and with education. People in their 40s bested everyone with 44 words, while 16- to 19-year-olds averaged 39 words.

In 1967, a research group developed scores for letters A through Y (X and Z were excluded) and found that F, A and S were among the "easiest" letters, allowing people to come up with the greatest number of words.

Source

Tom Tombaugh, a psychology professor at Carleton University in Ottawa, and colleagues tested 1,300 individuals who had no cognitive impairment. Their results were published in a 1999 article, "Normative Data Stratified By Age And Education For Two Measures Of Verbal Fluency," which appeared in the Archives of Clinical Neuropsychology

Remember The Milk

What it measures: Short-term memory

Shopping list

2 slices veal	10 bus tickets
1 lb. ham	1 box matches
1 salami	3 white envelopes
3 oz. Gorgonzola	1 box cookies
3 oz. prunes	1 bottle dish soap
2 cups cherries	1 quart milk
1 bottle water	2 turkey thighs
1 lb. sugar	1 newspaper
4 sandwiches	

Test
Look at the shopping list above. Study it carefully for five minutes, and then cover up the list. See how many of the items you can write down - both name and quantity - in five minutes.

Score
On average:
Sixty-to-80-year-olds recalled nine items.
Twenty- to-35 year- olds averaged 14 items.

Good to know :
This study found that if people practiced, they could improve their memory.

Source
Elena Cavallini and colleagues from the Universita di Pavia in Italy tested 60 individuals for their 2003 study, "Aging and everyday memory," which was published in the Archives of Gerontology and Geriatrics.

WORDS

8-Foot Up-and-Go

What it measures: Agility, dynamic balance

Test

Time how long it takes to stand from a seated position, walk 8 feet, turn around and walk back to the starting point and sit down.

Scores

Typical scores for men aged:

> 60-64: 3.8 to 5.6 seconds
>
> 65-69: 4.3 to 5.7 seconds
>
> 70-74: 4.2 to 6.0 seconds
>
> 75-79: 4.6 to 7.2 seconds
>
> 80-84: 5.2 to 7.6 seconds

Typical scores for women aged:

> 60-64: 4.4 to 6.0 seconds
>
> 65-69: 4.8 to 6.4 seconds
>
> 70-74: 4.9 to 7.1 seconds
>
> 75-79: 5.2 to 7.4 seconds
>
> 80-84: 5.7 to 8.7 seconds

Good to know

Taking more than nine seconds means you may be at risk for falls and should consider seeking assistance getting on or off a bus or getting up from a seated position.

Source

Jessie Jones and Roberta Rikli, kinesiology professors at California State University at Fullerton, published the Senior Fitness Test Manual in 2001 to assess older adults' abilities to perform daily tasks. The performance standards are based on their national study of more than 7,000 Americans.

❖

Strike A Pose

What it measures: Balance

Test

Stand on both feet, eyes closed. Right-handed folk, raise the left foot; lefties, raise the right, about six inches off the floor, bending the knee at a 45-degree angle. Then start the timer. As soon as you sway, open your eyes or touch the floor, stop the clock. Do this test three times and average your score.

Score

    50-year-olds should aim to balance for 9 seconds;

    60-yearolds, balance for 7 seconds;

    70-year-olds, balance for 4 seconds.

Good to know

Your ability to balance is a good indicator of risk of future falls.

Source

RealAge, an online resource developed by medical writers, epidemiologists and physicians, featured this test for age groups ranging from 25 to 70. See www.realage.com/shape-up-slimdown/ workout-center/ improve-your-balance.

Left-Right-Left

What it measures: Proprioception, or your sense of where you are in relation to your surroundings.

Test
For 30 seconds, march in place, eyes closed. Then open your eyes and see if you've moved from your original position.

Score
Although this test lacks age-related scores, if you were unable to stay in one place or if you are turned in a different direction, you may have proprioception problems.

Good to know
Proprioception allows us to do two things at the same time, without looking. For example, we rely on this sense to open a kitchen drawer while watching a boiling pot, or when we keep our eyes on the road while turning on the windshield wipers. This sense diminishes as people age. You can improve your proprioception by working on your balance.

Source
Gabi Redford, editorial projects manager for AARP the Magazine, suggested this task to the Chronicle during a phone interview.

✳

Wait ... Wait ... Go!

What it measures: Response time

Test

Go to www.topend sports.com/testing/rection-timer,hym. Follow the instructions to react quickly when the screen changes color. (This website also provides lots of information about reaction time.)

Score

Different sites for testing reaction speed have different measures of good scores, though most don't seem to provide age-related parameters for a good score.

Good to know

Reacting quickly to environmental changes is vital to driving and other everyday activities.

Sources

Other sites providing information on reaction time and testing include: www.humanbenchmark.com/tests/reactiontime/index.php, and www.math-isfun.com/games/reaction-time.htm.

Lions And Tigers And Bears

What it measures: Semantic fluency, mental organization, short-term memory

Test

How many animals can you list within a minute? No proper nouns, repeats or variations of the same word. (You can't use "lion" and "lions.")

Score

On average:

50 -to- 59-year-olds named 20 animals.

60 -to-69-year-olds named 18 animals.

70 -to-79-year-olds named 16 animals.

80 -to-89-year-olds named 14 animals.

90 -to-95-year-olds named 13 animals.

Good to know

Scores decreased with age. Younger minds generated the most animal names. Sixteen-to-19-year-olds listed 22 animals.

Source:

Study of 1,300 individuals by Carleton University in Ottawa, Canada. This exercise is found in several neuropsychological test batteries to assess semantic fluency.

✳

In the game of "Situation Puzzles," a mysterious situation is presented to a group of players, who must then try to find out what's going on by asking questions. The person presenting the situation can only answer "yes" or "no" to questions (or occasionally say "irrelevant").

Situation Puzzles

In telling a group of players a "situation," the presenter can add or remove details, either to make getting the answer harder or easier, or simply to throw in red herrings. Situation Puzzles are interactive games--that's what distinguishes them from riddles or logic puzzles. It's gaming at its best: asking questions to gradually gather the information that leads to the solution.

Comment: Life continually presents situations which require interpretation. Sometimes we can't solve the mystery and must either guess at a solution or let life go on by without ever discovering reality. Religion is sometimes like that. Sometimes it takes all the faith we have to accept a happening and move on.

Here's a situation: A man lives on the twelfth floor of an apartment building. Every morning he takes the elevator down to the lobby and leaves the building. In the evening, he gets into the elevator, and, if there is someone else in the elevator or if it was raining that day -- he goes back to his floor directly. However, if there is nobody else in the elevator and it hasn't rained, he goes to the 10th floor and walks up two flights of stairs to his room.

How come?

Answer: The man is a little person. He can't reach the upper elevator buttons, but he can ask people to push them for him. He can also push the elevator buttons with his umbrella.

If you want to explore more Situation Puzzles, just Google the words.

WORDS

Stumper

See if you can figure out what these words have in common:

1 Banana
2 Dresser
3 Grammar
4 Potato
5 Revive
6 Uneven
7 Assess

Answer: *No, it's not that they all have at least two double letters. In all of the words listed, take the first letter, place it at the end of the word and then spell it backwards.*

It'll be the same word!

WORDS

RELIGIOUS STUFF

God vs. Science
Computer generated drawing
© Rafi 2011

WORDS

The Problem Science has with Religion
God vs. Science

"Let me explain the problem science has with religion." The atheist professor of philosophy pauses before his class and then asks one of his new students to stand.

"You're a Christian, aren't you, son?"

"Yes sir," the student says.

"So you believe in God?"

"Absolutely."

"Is God good?"

"Sure! God's good."

"Is God all-powerful? Can God do anything?"

"Yes."

"Are you good or evil?"

"The Bible says I'm evil."

The professor grins knowingly. "Aha! The Bible!" He considers for a moment. "Here's one for you. Let's say there's a sick person over here and you can cure him. You can do it. Would you help him? Would you try?"

"Yes sir, I would."

"So you're good...!"

"I wouldn't say that."

"But why not say that? You'd help a sick and maimed person if you could. Most of us would if we could. But God doesn't."

The student does not answer, so the professor continues. "He doesn't, does he? My brother was a Christian who died of cancer, even though he prayed to Jesus to heal him. How is this Jesus good? Can you answer that one?"

The student remains silent. "No, you can't, can you?" the professor says. He takes a sip of water from a glass on his desk to give the student time to relax. "Let's start again, young fella. Is God good?"

"Er... yes," the student says.

"Is Satan good?"

The student doesn't hesitate on this one. "No."

"Then where does Satan come from?"

The student falters, "From God."

"That's right. God made Satan, didn't he? Tell me, son, is there evil in this world?"

"Yes, sir..."

"Evil's everywhere, isn't it? And God did make everything, correct?"

"Yes."

"So who created evil?" The professor continued, "If God created everything, then God created evil, since evil exists, and the principle that our works define who we are, then God is evil."

Again, the student has no answer.

"Is there sickness? Immorality? Hatred? Ugliness? All these terrible things, do they exist in this world?"

The student squirms on his feet. "Yes."

"So who created them?"

The student does not answer again, so the professor repeats his question. "Who created them?"

There is still no answer. Suddenly, the lecturer breaks away to pace in front of the classroom. The class is mesmerized. "Tell me," he continues onto another student. "Do you believe in Jesus Christ, son?"

The student's voice betrays him and cracks. "Yes, professor, I do."

The old man stops pacing. "Science says you have five senses you use to identify and observe the world around you. Have you ever seen Jesus?"

"No sir. I've never seen Him."

Then tell us if you've ever heard your Jesus?"

"No, sir, I have not."

"Have you ever felt your Jesus, tasted your Jesus or smelt your Jesus? Have you ever had any sensory perception of Jesus Christ, or God, for that matter?"

"No, sir, I'm afraid I haven't."

"Yet you still believe in him?"

"Yes."

"According to the rules of empirical, testable, demonstrable protocol, science says your God doesn't exist... What do you say to that, son?"

"Nothing," the student replies... "I only have my faith."

"Yes, faith," the professor repeats. "And that is the problem science has with God. There is no evidence, only faith."

The student stands quietly for a moment, before asking a question of his own. "Professor, is there such thing as heat? "

"Yes."

"And is there such a thing as cold?"

"Yes, son, there's cold too."

"No sir, there isn't."

The professor turns to face the student, obviously interested. The room suddenly becomes very quiet.

The student begins to explain, "You can have lots of heat, even more heat, super-heat, mega-heat, unlimited heat, white heat, a little heat or no heat, but we don't have anything called "cold." We can hit down to 458 degrees below zero, which is no heat, but we can't

go any further after that. There is no such thing as cold; otherwise we would be able to go colder than the lowest minus 458 degrees. Every body or object is susceptible to study when it has or transmits energy, and heat is what makes a body or matter have or transmit energy. Absolute zero (-458 F.) is the total absence of heat. You see, sir, cold is only a word we use to describe the absence of heat. We cannot measure cold. Heat we can measure in thermal units because heat is energy. Cold is not the opposite of heat, sir, just the absence of it."

Silence across the room. A pen drops somewhere in the classroom, sounding like a hammer.

"What about darkness, professor. Is there such a thing as darkness?"

"Yes," the professor replies without hesitation. "What is night if it isn't darkness?"

"You're wrong again, sir. Darkness is not something; it is the absence of something. You can have low light, normal light, bright light, flashing light, but if you have no light constantly you have nothing, and it's called darkness, isn't it? That's the meaning we use to define the word.
In reality, darkness isn't. If it were, you would be able to make darkness darker, wouldn't you?"

The professor begins to smile at the student in front of him. This will be a good semester. "So what point are you making, young man?"

"Yes, professor. My point is your philosophical premise is flawed to start with, and so your conclusion must also be flawed.

The professor's face cannot hide his surprise this time. "Flawed? Can you explain how?"

152

"You are working on the premise of duality," the student explains. "You argue that there is life and then there's death; a good God and a bad God. You are viewing the concept of God as something finite, something we can measure.

"Sir, science can't even explain a thought. It uses electricity and magnetism, but has never seen, much less fully understood either one. To view death as the opposite of life is to be ignorant of the fact that death cannot exist as a substantive thing. Death is not the opposite of life, just the absence of it. Now tell me, professor, do you teach your students that they evolved from a monkey?"

"If you are referring to the natural evolutionary process, young man, yes, of course I do."

"Have you ever observed evolution with your own eyes, sir?"

The professor begins to shake his head, still smiling, as he realizes where the argument is going. A very good semester, indeed.

"Since no one has ever observed the process of evolution at work and cannot even prove that this process is an ongoing endeavor, are you not teaching your opinion, sir? Are you now not a scientist, but a preacher?"

The class is in uproar. The student remains silent until the commotion has subsided. "To continue the point you were making earlier, let me give you an example of what I mean." The student looks around the room. "Is there anyone in the class who has ever seen the professor's brain?"

The class breaks out into laughter. "Is there anyone here who has ever heard the professor's brain, felt the professor's brain, touched or smelt the professor's brain? No one appears to have done so. So, according to the established rules of empirical, stable, demonstrable protocol, science says that you have no brain, with all due respect, sir. So if science says you have no brain, how can we trust your lectures, sir?"

Now the room is silent. The professor just stares at the student, his face unreadable. Finally, after what seems an eternity, the old man answers. "I guess you'll have to take them on faith."

"You accept that there is faith, and, in fact, faith exists with life," the student continues. "Now, sir, is there such a thing as evil?"

Now uncertain, the professor responds, "Of course, there is. We see evil every day. It is in the daily example of man's inhumanity to man. It is in the multitude of crime and violence everywhere in the world. These manifestations are nothing else but evil."

To this the student replied, "Evil does not exist, sir, or at least it does not exist unto itself. Evil is simply the absence of God. It is just like darkness and cold, a word that man has created to describe the absence of God. God did not create evil. Evil is the result of what happens when man does not have God's love present in his heart. It's like the cold that comes when there is no heat or the darkness that comes when there is no light."

The professor sat down.

I don't know who wrote this story, it came through email. If you read this little piece all the way through, you probably had a smile on your face when you finished. P.S: the student was Albert Einstein. Albert Einstein wrote a book titled **God vs. Science in 1921.**

Billy Graham and Albert Einstein

In January 2000, leaders in Charlotte, North Carolina, invited the great evangelist and their favorite son, Billy Graham, to a luncheon in his honor. Billy initially hesitated to accept the invitation because he struggles with Parkinson's disease. But the Charlotte leaders said, "We don't expect a major address. Just come and let us honor you." So he agreed.

After wonderful things were said about him, Dr. Graham stepped to the rostrum, looked at the crowd, and said, "I'm reminded today of Albert Einstein, the great physicist who this month has been honored by Time magazine as the Man of the Century. Einstein was once traveling from Princeton on a train when the conductor came down the aisle, punching the tickets of every passenger. When he came to Einstein, Einstein reached in his vest pocket. He couldn't find his ticket, so he reached in his trouser pockets. It wasn't there. He looked in his briefcase but couldn't find it. Then he looked in the seat beside him. He still couldn't find it. The conductor said, "Dr. Einstein, I know who you are. We all know who you are.

I'm sure you bought a ticket. Don't worry about it." Einstein nodded appreciatively.

The conductor continued down the aisle punching tickets. As he was ready to move to the next car, he turned around and saw the great physicist down on his hands and knees looking under his seat for his ticket. The conductor rushed back and said, "Dr. Einstein, Dr. Einstein, don't worry, I know who you are; no problem. You don't need a ticket. I'm sure you bought one."

Einstein looked at him and said, 'Young man, I too, know who I am. What I don't know is where I'm going!"

Having said that, Billy Graham continued, "See the suit I'm wearing? It's a brand new suit. My children and my grandchildren are telling me I've gotten a little slovenly in my old age. I used to be a bit more fastidious. So I went out and bought a new suit for this luncheon and one more occasion. You know what that occasion is? This is the suit in which I'll be buried. But when you hear I'm dead, I don't want you to remember the suit I'm wearing. I want you to remember this: I not only know who I am. I also know where I'm going."

God's Answers

You Say	God Says	Bible Verse
It's impossible	All things are possible	*Luke 18:27*
I'm too tired	I will give you rest	*Matthew 11:28-30*
Nobody really loves me	I love you	*John 3:16; 3:24*
I can't go on	My grace is sufficient	*II Col. 12:9*
I can't figure things out	I will direct your steps	*Proverbs 3:5-6*
I can't do it	You can do all things	*Philippians 4:13*
I'm afraid	I have not given you a spirit of fear	*II Timothy 1:7*
I'm always worried and frustrated	Cast all your cares on me	*1 Peter 5:7*
I'm not smart enough	I give you wisdom	*I Corinthians 1:30*
I feel alone	I will never leave or forsake you	*Hebrews 13:5*

If you're like most of us, there was a time when you doubted some of the things everyone else believed without question. If you're one of those persons who still wonder every once in a while, this piece is for you.

What If Everything You Believe Is Wrong?

There are some things we know to be true. Occasionally, we discover something we thought true turns out not to be. And there are always unanswered questions. Some of our questions are resolved by expanded knowledge. The answer to some questions we find unacceptable, unbelievable. .

How do we know for certain our beliefs are true? What if, suddenly, you find out something you've always thought was dependently true, wasn't?

Even with all our life experiences, there are still things we cannot say are either true or false—we are uncertain.

Here's something else: even with substantial knowledge of the present, predicting the future accurately is not easy. For example, can you say with certainty who will go to heaven? When we do try to base an action on what we think will happen (like placing trust in someone), we are sometimes disappointed.

Uncertainty is everywhere. You can't escape it. It is not restricted to religious doubts. In fact, a whole branch of philosophy has developed around not knowing everything. It's called, aptly enough, "Uncertainty Philosophy."

Presented with options, you and I will probably say we resolve uncertain issues based on information we have— knowledge-guided decisions —even though we may not have all relevant information." However, there are other ways uncertain issues are resolved. *(See the chart below.)*

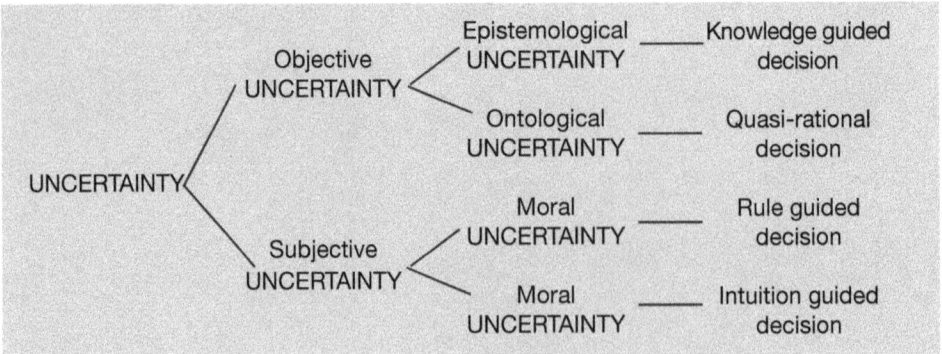

Chart by Dennis Lindley, Understanding Uncertainty (2006). The book examines the many diverse forms of uncertainty and includes examples where the truth is genuinely unknown. For example, "The defendant is guilty," "It will rain tomorrow," "A card drawn from a shuffled pack will be an ace," or "the flight will arrive tomorrow on time." For the type of book it is, it is written in relatively-easy-to-read prose.

WORDS

We like to believe knowledge is the basis for the decisions we make even though we sometimes are in error. But what do we do when another option representing possible truth presents itself and we want to make the right decision?

Rules make decision making easier, as does having lots of information. Some of us depend on our gut to guide us. Before you give up in frustration (uncertainty?), you should know **the major points of this "uncertainty philosophy" are primary to your belief system.**

Surprised?

You probably will not dispute the statement that humans sometimes make mistakes. This belief, known philosophically as *epistemology,* is one half of a serious discussion of uncertainty. The other half, *fallibilism,* holds there is no way we can know the mind of God, and, therefore, the things we hold true about God may not be what He/She meant at all. The statement, *"Without fear of contradiction, this is what God says,"* expresses the two uncertainty ideas, *epistemology and fallibilism.*

Hard to get with it? Don't give up, stay with me.

Epistemology is the view that humans might make a mistake. *Fallibilism* is the belief that human beings cannot know the mind of God.

So our beliefs about God might be mistaken, **and,** smart as we are, we're not smart enough to understand God. Combine the two and you have uncertainty (I think!).

But wait a moment: fallibilism also holds that truth is truth until another truth comes along.

Dennis Lindley demonstrates the way uncertainty works in this religious illustration from his book, *Understanding Uncertainty,* (altered slightly for this article): *"For some Christians, Jesus is the Son of God. This is a certain statement based on faith. For atheists, it is an uncertain statement that cannot be proved. For agnostics, it is unknown and unknowable—they acknowledge they do not know.*

Fallibists believe that absolute certainty about knowledge is impossible. We get new information every day, some of which changes older beliefs. (No one believes today the world is flat!) Fallibilism does not imply the need to abandon current knowledge, and it is not required to have logically conclusive justifications for what one knows. Rather, **it is the belief that new information might change older beliefs. So, the things we take as solid might turn out to be false because new information comes along.**

Who could argue with that?

Some suggest that epistemological fallibilism is a contradiction in that it is in itself an absolute knowledge claim. In other words, the statement, "This much is certain: nothing is certain," is an unconnected statement that could not be true. *However, the easy way to handle this statement is to agree (think) the issue of concern (whatever it is) is true until it is proven certainly false.*

Epistemology is a branch of philosophy that studies the nature of knowledge, its presuppositions and foundations, and its extent and validity. It accepts the view that **all human beings are liable to error.**

And there's the rub: What if we are in error?

If you want to split hairs, some fallibilists make an exception for things that are obviously true ("axiomatically true" is the term fallibilists use, citing examples such as mathematical and logical knowledge). However, other fallibilists disagree with that premise on the basis that, even if axiomatic systems are in a sense infallible, we humans are still capable of error when working with these systems.

Just for the fun of it, the next time you discuss the existence of God with your friends (and you're all still sober), ask them if it is possible to **prove any truth with certainty?** (It's the old conundrum, "How do you know true is true?")

Philosophers respond to this "true is true" type of question with the *Münchhausen Trilemma,* which involves making a decision from three equally unsatisfying options:

• The *circular* argument, in which theory and proof support each other (i.e., we repeat ourselves at some point),

• The *regressive* argument, in which each proof requires a further proof, ad infinitum (i.e., we just keep giving proofs, presumably forever), and

• The *axiomatic* argument, which rests on accepted precepts (i.e., we agree on some bedrock assumption or certainty and work from there).

The **trilemma,** then, is a decision chosen from among the three equally unsatisfying options.

Moral Fallibilism holds that objectively true moral standards may exist, but that they cannot be reliably or conclusively determined true by humans. Think of it like this: morality *can be a conflict between differing objective moralities.* This means that more than one belief may be thought to be correct. For example, "Christians are going to heaven but Muslims and Buddhists are not." Or, "Muslims are going to heaven, but Christians and Buddhists are not." Who can really say with certainty who is right or wrong?

Moral Fallibilism is a part of the "Certainty" concept (there are about 15 philosophies under the Certainty umbrella). In their own way, all address the questions:

• What is knowledge?
• How is knowledge acquired?
• How do we know what we know?

The philosophical concept of certainty is important if you're religious because it goes to the heart of your beliefs. The question boils down to "How do you know for certain there is a God?" Alternatively, "How do you know your beliefs are true?" Really now, how do you prove relational notions like *truth, belief,* and *justification*?

OK, there you have it: Epistemology and Fallibism. What do you think?

If this kind of stuff turns you on, you would enjoy the book, "Plato and a Platypus Walk Into a Bar" by Thomas Cathcart and Daniel Klein by Penguin Books. It is a delightful explanation of philosophy through jokes.
"Understanding Uncertainty," Wikipedia, and "Plato and a Platypus Walk into a Bar" are the reference sources for this article. I think I understand what I've written, but you never know!

WORDS

Certainty

Do you have beliefs that are absolutely certain, that do not consider the possibility of alternative statements? Do you have beliefs so firm they eliminate any discussion regarding other beliefs and/or the contradictions of science?

You're certain, then. Certainty can be defined as either:

- Perfect knowledge that has total security from error, or
- The mental state of being without doubt.

Are you that way about anything?

Objectively defined, certainty is total continuity and validity of all foundational inquiry to the highest degree of precision. Something is certain only if no skepticism can occur. Philosophy seeks this state. Certainty is, for most of us, a religious issue.

It is widely held by philosophers that certainty is a failed historical enterprise. Physicist and Philosopher Carlo Rovelli said, "Certainty, in real life, is useless or often damaging." He believes the idea of having "total security from error" is impossible in practice, and a "complete lack of doubt is undesirable."

What does that statement say about your religious beliefs?

The certainty issue is raised by the philosophical question: "Does inductive reasoning lead to knowledge?" Philosophically, inductive reasoning is much more subtle than the simple progression from particular/individual instances to wider generalizations. *An inductive logical argument indicates some degree of probability for a particular conclusion (generalizing) but does not exclude other possibilities. Inductive reasoning suggests truth but does not ensure it (presupposing).*

Generalizing about something is based on a number of observations (for example, the classical inference that "all the swans we have seen are white, and therefore all swans are white." But what happens with the discovery of black swans?)

Presupposing is the belief that a sequence of events in the future will occur as has always occurred in the past (for example, the laws of physics will hold as they have always been observed to hold).

Is Rovelli right? Is "total security from error" impossible in practice? More importantly, is complete "lack of doubt" undesirable?

Do you see where this uncertainty discussion is headed? There's lots more philosophical stuff written on this subject. If you want to resolve this conundrum, good luck. You'll need it,

This discussion has been going on for a long time. Henry Brooks Adams, (1838–1918), a U.S. historian, wrote regarding the attitude of religion towards science: "If there is still a feeling of hostility between them, it is no longer the fault of religion. There have been times when the church seemed afraid, but she is so no longer. Analyze, dissect, use your microscope or your spectrum till the last atom of matter is reached; reflect and refine till the last element of thought is made clear. The church now knows with the certainty of science what she once knew only by the certainty of faith, that you will find enthroned behind all thought and matter only one central idea which the church has never ceased to embody: I AM!"

He's certainly certain. Are you?

As senior adults, we probably think more about life's ending than we do about its beginning. That's normal. Many older men and women say their beliefs about creation were acquired as children and haven't changed much. But as we age, life's ending consumes a great deal of our thoughts.

This non-technical article summarizes current theories regarding the creation of the earth, billions of years ago, in preparation for the appearance of man and woman. It proceeds to a recognition of end-of-life issues and how seniors can help those who survive them by preparing for their death and preserving for the future items of importance.

A part of our belief system includes the creation of the earth and, subsequently, man and woman. Like many of our convictions, as we matured, we enlarged our perspectives and changed the way we saw the world when we were young. We have no quarrel with those who say everything is continuing to change—we see it everywhere. How God performs his miracles remain mysteries—some of which we are just gradually understanding. However, science has convinced us that earth has been around a long time. The world, and those of us who dwell on it, is not the same as it was billions of years ago. Earth is, you know, the only known home-to-life in the universe. It's the third planet from the Sun and the densest and fifth-largest of the eight planets in our Solar System. It's an amazing place. As far as we know, it's unique to everything else in the cosmos.

Scientists say life forms appeared on our planet more than three billion years ago, evolving over time from the most basic of microbes into a dazzling array of complexity, ready for human habitation. How on earth does the beginning of earth have anything at all to do with end of life questions? Being able to talk about beginnings is a way to transition into a more serious discussion of life's end. It's something everyone should be interested in.

There are at least seven theories from diverse scientific disciplines about how it all began. Whichever theory is right, God was essential to it. There's no doubt about it. But a lot of stuff had to happen to get Earth ready for man.

Which one of the following seven theories about the Earth's growth do you like?

- **Electric Sparks** can generate amino acids and sugars, key building blocks, from an atmosphere loaded with water, methane, ammonia and hydrogen. The famous 1953 Miller-Urey experiment suggests that lightning might have helped create the building blocks of life on earth in its early days, and over millions of years, larger and more complex molecules formed.

- **Community Clay** The first molecules of life might have met on clay, according to an idea put forth by organic chemist Alexander Graham Cairns-Smith at the University of Glasgow in Scotland. These surfaces might not only have concentrated organic compounds together, but also helped organize them into patterns much like our genes do now. DNA

WORDS

is integral to this theory. The main role of DNA is to store information on how other molecules should be arranged. Genetic sequences in DNA are essentially instructions on how amino acids should be arranged in proteins. Cairns-Smith suggests that mineral crystals in clay could have arranged organic molecules into organized patterns. After a while, organic molecules took over this job and organized themselves.

- **The Deep-Sea Vent Theory** suggests that life may have begun at submarine hydrothermal vents, spewing key hydrogen-rich molecules. The deep sea rocky nooks could then have concentrated these molecules together and provided mineral catalysts for critical reactions. Even now, underwater vents rich in chemical and thermal energy, sustain vibrant ecosystems.

- **Chilly Ice** might have covered the oceans three billion years ago, as the sun was about a third less luminous than it is now. This layer of ice, possibly hundreds of feet thick, might have protected fragile organic compounds in the water below from ultraviolet light and destruction from cosmic impacts. The cold might have also helped these molecules survive longer, allowing key reactions to happen.

- **RNA World** Nowadays DNA needs proteins in order to form, and proteins require DNA to form, so how could these have formed without each other? The answer may be RNA. RNA can store information like DNA, serve as an enzyme-like protein, and help create both DNA and proteins. Later, DNA and proteins succeeded the "RNA World" because they are more efficient.

RNA still exists and performs several functions in organisms, including acting as an on-off switch for some genes. Unanswered is how RNA got here in the first place?

- **Simple Beginnings** Instead of developing from complex molecules such as RNA, life might have begun with smaller molecules interacting with each other in cycles of reactions. These molecules might have been contained in capsules akin to cell membranes, and over time evolved into more complex molecules that performed these reactions better than the smaller ones. This theory has been dubbed a "metabolism-first" model, in contrast to the "gene-first" model of the "RNA World" hypothesis.

- **Outer Space** Perhaps life did not begin on Earth at all, but was brought here from elsewhere in space, a notion known as *panspermia*. A number of Martian meteorites have been found on Earth, leading some researchers to suggest Mars-sent microbes started it all, potentially making us Martians originally. However, even if this concept were true, the question of how life began on Earth would then only change to how life began elsewhere in space.

(The creation theories were condensed from a research article written by Charles Choi, a freelance reporter. Email him at cgchot @sciwriter.us or go to his web site www.sciwriter.us.)

Which one of these theories is correct? Who knows? Scientists suggest using extreme caution on any choice that has not yet gone through rigorous peer review. But for casual discussions, they are perfect!

End-of-life Issues

We don't have to worry about life's beginnings, other than to speculate conversationally. However, there are real issues to contend with as our lives begin to wind down, and plenty of personal end-of-life questions that need answers. We're lucky that others have developed death planning checklists we can refer to and use to develop our own answers.

The steps to follow to prepare for the end of life are covered in logical order in John Leslie's book, "I'm Not Dead Yet." He suggests the first thing you should do is create a personal "Going Away" book where everything important can be filed and easily found. After you die the book becomes the first place your family will look for guidance and be able to follow your previously prepared instructions. To help, he includes a list of possible subjects for each section, including what to do immediately on your death.

After you've made your decisions, be sure someone knows what you have decided. File your written instructions in your Going Away book. It's even a good idea to give a copy of the critical documents to family members and a couple of friends. What you want done after you die should not be kept a secret. Don't file your instructions with your will; there's a chance what you want done won't be found until it's too late.

Put your book in a very visible place where everyone can find it. And, just to be sure, try to get family members to read and discuss your entries in the various sections.

Understanding the many complexities of the world and its mysteries may be impossible for most of us, but we will leave this world a better place because we've been here. Our greatest legacy will be compassion for those we leave behind. Making it easier for them to handle our end-of-life may be our greatest gift.

You Might Be Wrong

By Paul Thorn on the Music Fog bus .
From his album, "Pimps and Preachers"

Muslims Christians, Buddhists and Jews
Got their own version of the truth.
There's a line in the sand,
There's a war goin' on.
They forgot to remember
You might be wrong.
Carry your faith
Everywhere you go
Mix it with love and let it show.
But keep your mind open
As you move along,
And always remember,
You might be wrong.

Why do we argue?
Why do we fight?
Everybody thinks
God's on their side.
Count to ten
Before you throw a stone.
Whatever you believe,
You might be wrong

Don't cut me off.
Don't say we're through
Just because
I don't agree with you.
You see flowers grow
Where seeds of love are sown.
You could be right.
You might be wrong.

Why do we argue?
Why do we fight?
Everybody thinks
God's on their side.
Count to ten
Before you throw a stone.
Whatever you believe,
You might be wrong

What's on the other side of life?
I won't know until the day I die.
If you feel insecure
You are not alone
Everybody knows
You might be wrong.

Why do we argue?
Why do we fight?
Everybody thinks
God's on their side.
Count to ten
Before you throw a stone.
Whatever you believe,
You might be wrong

After reading this, you'll never look at a deck of cards the same way.

A Deck of Cards

It was quiet that day; the guns, the mortars, and land mines for some reason hadn't been heard. The young soldier knew it was Sunday, the holiest day of the week. As he was sitting there, he got out an old deck of cards and laid them out across his bunk.

Just then an army sergeant came in and said, *"Why aren't you with the rest of the platoon?"*

The soldier replied, *"I thought I would stay behind and spend some time with the Lord."*

The sergeant said, *"Looks to me like you're going to play cards."*

The soldier said, *"No, sir. You see, since we are not allowed to have Bibles or other spiritual books in this country, I've decided to talk to the Lord by studying this deck of cards.*

The sergeant asked in disbelief, *"How will you do that?"*

"You see the Ace, Sergeant? It reminds me that there is only one God.

The Two represents the two parts of the Bible, Old and New Testaments.

The Three represents the Father, Son, and the Holy Ghost.

The Four stands for the Four Gospels: Matthew, Mark, Luke and John.

The Five is for the five virgins; there were ten but only five of them were glorified.

The Six is for the six days it took God to create the Heavens and Earth.

The Seven is for the day God rested after making His Creation.

The Eight is for the family of Noah and his wife, their three sons and their wives -- the eight people God spared from the flood that destroyed the Earth.

The Nine is for the lepers that Jesus cleansed of leprosy. He cleansed ten, but nine never thanked Him.

The Ten represents the Ten Commandments that God handed down to Mosses on tablets made of stone.

The Jack is a reminder of Satan, one of God's first angels, but he got kicked out of heaven for his sly and wicked ways and is now the joker of eternal hell.

The Queen stands for the Virgin Mary.

The King stands for Jesus, for he is the King of all kings.

When I count the dots on all the cards, I come up with 365, one for every day of the year.

There are a total of 52 cards in a deck; each is a week - 52 weeks in a year.

The four suits represent the four seasons: Spring, Summer, Fall and Winter. Each suit has thirteen cards -- there are exactly thirteen weeks in a quarter.

So when I want to talk to God and thank Him, I just pull out this old deck of cards and they remind me of all that I have to be thankful for."

The sergeant just stood there. After a minute, with tears in his eyes, he said, *"Soldier, can I borrow that deck of cards?"*

There's some information here you probably didn't know and references to religions you may never have heard of. The data from the sources has been edited for brevity and, hopefully, easier understanding. It's pretty interesting.

Religious Groups

Religious traditions are most often arranged by historical origin and influence, as follows:

- **Abrahamic religions** (originated in the Middle East) are the largest group and consist mainly of Christianity, Islam, Judaism and the Baha'i Faith. They are named for the patriarch Abraham and are unified by the practice of monotheism (the belief in the existence of one god). Around 3.5 billion people are followers of Abrahamic religions and are spread widely around the world, apart from the regions around Southeast Asia. Several Abrahamic organizations are vigorous proselytizers.

- **Indian religions** (originated in Greater India) tend to share a number of key concepts, such as dharma and karma. They are of the most influence across the Indian subcontinent, East Asia, Southeast Asia, and in isolated parts of Russia. The main Indian religions are Hinduism, Jainism, Buddhism and Sikhism.

- **East Asian religions** make use of the concept of Tao (in Chinese) or Do (in Japanese or Korean). Some scholars believe the main groups, Taoism and Confucianism, to be non-religious in nature.

- **Africa** (originated in Central and West Africa) accepted Jews who were exiled from Israel in the sixth century B.C. The Jews combined their practices with the traditional religions of Central and West Africa. Then, as a result of the 16th to 18th centuries' slave trading, their religious practices were brought to the Americas by the slaves.

- **Indigenous ethnic religions,** formerly found on every continent, are now marginalized by the major organized faiths, but persist as undercurrents of folk religion.

- **Iranian religions** originated in Iran and include Zoroastrianism, Yazdanism, Ahl-e Haqq and historical traditions of Gnosticism (Mandaeism, Manichaeism). It has significant overlaps with Abrahamic traditions, e.g. in Sufism and in recent movements such as Bâbism and the Bahâ'i Faith.

- **New religious movement** is the term applied to any religious faith which has emerged since the 19th century, often reconciling contrary beliefs, often melding practices of various schools of thought, or re-interpreting or reviving aspects of older traditions. Examples are the Hindu reform movements, Eckankar, Ayyavazhi, Pentecostalism, polytheistic reconstructionism, and so forth.

Major World Religions

(As determined by the number of adherents)

Another way to define a major religion is by the number of current adherents. The numbers by religion shown below are computed by a combination of census reports and population surveys in countries where religion data is not collected in census. Results can vary widely, depending on the way questions are phrased, the definitions of religion used, and the bias of the agencies or organizations conducting the survey. Informal or unorganized religions are especially difficult to count.

There is no consensus among researchers as to the best methodology for determining the religiosity profile of the world's population. (see the Wikipedia article, Major World Religions, for a description of the various profile options)

The religious population numbers below are computed by a combination of census reports, random surveys, and self-reported attendance numbers. The numbers are estimates only, but accepted by scholars as reasonably accurate.

1. Christianity: 2 billion
2. Islam: 1.3 billion
3. Hinduism: 900 million
4. Secular/Nonreligious/Agnostic/Atheist: 850 million
5. Buddhism: 360 million
6. Chinese traditional religion: 225 million
7. Primal-indigenous: 150 million
8. African Traditional and Diasporic: 95 million
9. Sikhism: 23 million
10. Juche: 19 million
11. Spiritism: 14 million
12. Judaism: 14 million
13. Baha'i: 6 million
14. Jainism: 4 million
15. Shinto: 4 million
16. Cao Dai: 3 million
17. Tenrikyo: 2.4 million
18. Neo-Paganism: 1 million
19. Unitarian-Universalism: 800 thousand
20. Rastafarianism: 700 thousand
21. Scientology: 600 thousand
22. Zoroastrianism: 150 thousand

Last modified September 2002. Sizes shown are approximate estimates, mainly for the purpose of ordering the groups. Note: The first four groups represent over five billion adherents and are clearly the major religions..

WORDS

Trends in the Number of Believers

The demographics of religion have been changing rather slowly for years. Based on world events, it appears change will occur more rapidly in the years ahead.

There are two major indicators of decline in active participation in Christian religious life:

- declining recruitment for the priesthood and monastic life, as well as

- diminishing attendance at church.

Some countries with a historically large Christian population have experienced a significant decline in the numbers of professed active Christians. However, there are some bright spots. Since the 19th century, large areas of sub-Saharan Africa have been converted to Christianity. This area of the world has the highest population growth rate, so there is an upsurge in Christian membership possible.

In Western civilization, there has been an increase in

- the people who say they not controlled by a religious body, or

- those who say they are not concerned with religious or spiritual matters but have a strong interest in or concern for human welfare, values, and dignity.

In many countries, governments discourage religion. As a result, it is difficult to count the actual number of believers. However, after the collapse of communism in numerous countries of Eastern Europe and the former Soviet Union, religious life has been experiencing resurgence there.

Studies conducted by the Pew Research Center found that, generally, poorer nations had a larger proportion of citizens who found religion to be very important than richer nations. The United States and Kuwait are exceptions to this finding. Membership in a religion can grow in numbers because of conversion or because of higher birth rates in a religious group (assuming that children take on the religion of their parents). Religions in some countries grow because of immigration. So "fastest growing" could refer to the religion:

- Whose absolute number of adherents is growing the fastest (by whatever means).

- That is growing fastest in terms of percentage growth per year (by whatever means).

- That is gaining the greatest number of converts.

- That is gaining the greatest number of associative members

The World Christian Database contains data on numbers and growth of religions. *References* to *absolute numbers tend to favor the larger religions; percentage growth favors the smaller ones.*

% GROWTH OF RELIGIONS BY PERIOD

1970-1985	1990-2000	2000-2005
3.65% - Bahá'í Faith	2.65% - Zoroastrianism	1.84% - Islam
2.74% - Islam	2.28% - Bahá'í Faith	1.70% - Bahá'í Faith
2.30% - Hinduism	1.44% - Islam	1.62% - Sikhism
1.67% - Buddhism	1.87% - Sikhism	1.57% - Jainism
1.21% - Christianity	1.69% - Hinduism	1.52% - Hinduism
1.09% - Judaism	1.36% - Christianity	1.38% - Christianity
1.09% - Buddhism		
0.91% - Judaism		

Christian and Muslim faiths are competing for first place. The data below indicates Christian membership will exceed Muslim for the immediate future, but Muslim birth rates exceed Christian, so the gap is closing.

Estimated 2000			Projected 2005			Projected 2050		
Adherents		%	Adherents		%	Adherents		%
Christianity	1.999,563,838	33.0	3,016,670,052		33.4	3,652.564,342		35.5
Islam	1,188,242,789	19.6	2,184,875,653		26.1	2,629,281,610		28.0

The Carnegie Endowment for International Peace, using the 2000-2005 edition of the World Christian Database, concluded high birth rates were the main reason for growth; however, some of the growth of Christianity was also attributed to conversions. (see the Table on the next page).

170

WORDS

Growth of Selected Religions

1990-2000

Religion	Births	Conversions	New Adherents per year	Growth rate
Christianity	22,708,799	2,501,396	**25,210,195**	1.36%
Islam	21,723,118	865,558	**22,588,676**	2.13%
Hinduism	13,194,111	660,377	**13,854,488**	1.69%
Buddhism	3,530,918	156,609	**3,687,527**	1.09%
Sikhism	363,677	28,961	**392,638**	1.87%
Judaism	194,962	-70,447	**124,515**	0.91%
Baha'i Faith	117,158	26,333	**143,491**	2.28%
Confucianism	55,739	-11,434	**44,305**	0.73%
Jainism	74,539	-39,588	**34,951**	0.87%
Shinto	8,534	-40,527	**-31,993**	-1.09%
Taoism	25,397	-155	**25,242**	1.00%
Zoroastrianism	45,391	13,080	**58,471**	2.65%

The above table is based on data from the 2005 edition of Encyclopedia Britannica. Its figures for percentage growth come from the 1990 to 2000 version of the World Christian Database.

Religious Persecution in the World

The World Watch List ranks countries where persecution of Christians for religious reasons is worst. The compilation covers changes in two years to Christian denominations. The complete list covers 50 countries; only the worst 30 are shown in this article.

The data was developed by **Open Doors,** an organization whose main purpose is to deliver Bibles and Scripture resources to believers in the world's most restricted countries. (Their web site:www.opendoorsusa.com.)

The period for the chart is from November 1, 2009, through October 31, 2010. Rankings are compiled from a specially-designed questionnaire of 50 questions covering various aspects of religious freedom. A point value is then assigned depending on how each question is answered. The total number of points per country determines its position on the list.

According to the organization's writings, they ask questions like these to establish rankings:

- Does the constitution and/or national laws provide for freedom of religion?
- Are individuals allowed to convert to Christianity by law?
- The actual situation of individual Christians.
- Are Christians being killed because of their faith?
- Are Christians being sentenced to jail, labor camp or sent to a psychiatric hospital because of their faith?
- What is the role of the church in society?
- Do Christians have the freedom to print and distribute Christian literature?
- Are Christian publications censured or prohibited in this country?
- Are there other factors that may obstruct the freedom of religion in a country?
- Are Christian meeting places and/or Christian homes attacked because of anti-Christian motives?

Ranking of Religious Persecution by Country
Worst ranked highest

Rank	Country	Oct. 2010	Nov. 2009
1	North Korea	90.5	90.5
2	Iran	67.5	65.5
3	Afghanistan	66.0	61.5
4	Saudi Arabia	64.5	63.5
5	Somalia	64.0	62.5
6	Maldives	63.0	62.0
7	Yemen	60.0	60.5
8	Iraq	58.5	48.0
9	Uzbekistan	57.5	56.0
10	Laos	56.0	56.0
11	Pakistan	55.5	51.5
12	Eritrea	55.0	54.5
13	Mauritania	53.5	59.5
14	Bhutan	53.5	53.5
15	Turkmenistan	51.5	49.5
16	China	48.5	51.5
17	Qatar	48.5	48.0
18	Vietnam	48.0	46.0
19	Egypt	47.5	47.0
20	Chechnya	47.0	47.0
21	Comoros	46.5	48.5
22	Algeria	45.0	41.0
23	North nigeria	44.0	41.0
24	Azerbaijan	43.5	42.0
25	Libya	41.0	42.5
26	Omen	41.0	40.0
27	Burma/Myanmar	40.0	42.0
28	Kuwait	40.0	38.0
29	Brunei	39.5	38.5
30	Turkey	39.5	36.0

Professionals and Their Hymns

Dentist's Hymn:	*Crown Him with Many Crowns*
Weatherman's Hymn:	*There Shall Be Showers of Blessing*
Contractor's Hymn:	*The Church's One Foundation*
Tailor's Hymn:	*Holy, Holy, Holy*
Golfer's Hymn:	*There's a Green Hill Far Away*
Politician's Hymn:	*Standing on the Promises*
Optometrist's Hymn:	*Open My Eyes That I Might See*
IRS Agent's Hymn:	*I Surrender All*
Gossip's Hymn:	*Pass It On*
Electrician's Hymn:	*Send The Light*
Shopper's Hymn:	*Sweet By and By*
Realtor's Hymn:	*I've Got a Mansion*
Massage Therapists Hymn	*He Touched Me*
Doctor's Hymn:	*The Great Physician*

For those who speed on the highway:

45mph	*God Will Take Care of You*
55mph	*Guide Me, O Thou Great Jehovah*
65mph	*Nearer My God To Thee*
75mph	*Nearer Still Nearer*
85mph	*This World Is Not My Home*
95mph	*Lord, I'm Coming Home*
100 mph and over	*Precious Memories*

WORDS

A Prayer of Hope

Lord, you know better than I know myself, that I am growing older and will someday be old.

Keep me from getting talkative and particularly from the fatal habit of thinking I must say something on every subject and on every occasion. Release me from craving to try to straighten out everybody's affairs.

Make me thoughtful, but not moody. Helpful but not bossy.

With my vast store of wisdom, it seems a pity not to use it all, but You know, Lord, that I want a few friends at the end.

Keep my mind free from the recital of endless details; give me wings to get to the point.

Seal my lips from my many aches and pains. They are increasing and my love of rehearsing them is becoming sweeter as the years go by.

I ask for grace enough to listen to the tales of others' pains. Help me to endure them with patience.

Teach me the glorious lesson that it is occasionally possible that I will be mistaken.

Keep me reasonably sweet. I do not want to be a saint; some of them are hard to live with; but a sour old man or woman is one of the crowning works of the devil. Help me to extract all possible fun out of life. There are so many funny things around us and I don't want to miss any of them.

Amen.

This prayer is attributed to a 14th entury nun. It's been translated into modern English..